Using Hops

The Complete Guide to Hops for the Craft Brewer

by Mark Garetz

A HopTech Book

Using Hops
The Complete Guide to Hops for the Craft Brewer
by Mark Garetz
Copyright 1994 by Mark Garetz

First Edition

ISBN 0-9640785-0-3
Printed in the United Sates of America

Published by
HopTech
P.O. Box 2172
Danville, CA 94526

Direct all inquiries or orders to the above address.

Cover Photo of the hop cone by Ulrich Gampert.
(It's Nugget, in case you were wondering.)

Back Cover Photo of the author standing next to the
Hopland, CA sign by Lynnette Garetz.

Contents

v

Acknowledgements

I would like to acknowledge the following individuals and companies who have helped me in the preparation of this book:

Fritz Maytag, Phil Rogers and Alan Kornhauser from Anchor Brewing, Dave Wills, Gail Nickerson, Dr. Al Haunold, Dr. Michael Lewis, Glenn Tinseth, Jim Koch from the Boston Beer Company, Darren Whitcher, Sid Stafford from Mendocino Brewing, Roger Lind from Lind Brewing, Don and Lynne O'Connor, Ulrich Gampert, Dr. Terry Foster, Bob Regent, Micah Millspaw from Murphy's Creek Brewing, Bob Jones, Dr. George Fix, Mark Miller, Stephen Mallery and many more.

Many of these people spent long hours reviewing the manuscript. I am truly grateful for their efforts. Their help and input have improved the book immensely.

A special thanks is in order for the help and cooperation of the fine people at Hopunion USA, Inc.: Dr. Greg Lewis, Ralph Olson, Ralph Woodall and Marcie Shull-Desserault. They have provided hop variety data, pictures, samples and much more.

This book is dedicated to my wife Lynnette Garetz. Without her patience, understanding, encouragement and love, I would never have completed this book.

Introduction

Hops are one of the most important ingredients in beer. But if we examine most books on brewing, hops are never given more than a few pages of sketchy data. The advice on how to use them in brewing is even more scant, and sometimes of questionable value. *Using Hops* is the first book dedicated to the subject of hops with an emphasis on using them in homebrewing, but the microbrewer will benefit from much of the information as well.

Using Hops starts out with a general introduction to the subject of hops, and touches lightly on their use in brewing and other topics. Then it goes over the brewing and related information in greater detail. The reason for this approach is so that all of the terms and general definitions can be gotten out of the way so they won't clutter up the later chapters. On the other hand, in many places I've intentionally repeated some information rather than constantly referring you back to other chapters and sections. This does give a feeling of redundancy at times if you read the book straight through. But I suspect this book will be used primarily as a reference, and therefore I wanted each chapter or section to stand on its own wherever practical.

A section on *Growing Your Own Hops* has been included, written by Dave Wills of Freshops. Dave has been a supplier of hops to homebrewers for many years, as well as the source of most of the hop rhizomes (the part you plant to grow your own) available to homebrewers.

1

A few words should be mentioned about the style of this book and the sources of information it is based on. As for my personal writing style, I tend to shift back and forth between "I", "we" and the third person. Here's why: When I say "I" it means that what I am saying is my personal opinion, or is related to something I do or did, (an example is "When I add hops to my wort..."). When I say "we" it means me and you (the reader), and by extension, the entire craft brewing community (an example would be "when we add hops to wort..."). But sometimes I'll just say "When hops are added to wort..." or the like. Sometimes I like to pose questions I think you might be asking, such as, "OK. When do I add the hops to the wort?" In this case the "I" means "you" since I'm temporarily playing the part of reader!

I could have written this book in the dry, "academic" style, including reference numbers every few sentences. But I personally find reading that style of writing tedious (not to mention writing it!). That is not to say that there has been no investigation of the research that has been conducted in professional brewing circles. In fact, quite the opposite is true. Thousands of pages of scientific brewing literature have been reviewed in the research for this book, as well as many hours of interviews with brewers, hop suppliers and hop researchers. I have not blindly taken anything written in the homebrewing literature on faith - instead I have endeavored to make sure it agrees with other research. Anyway, I have used a more informal, conversational tone and eliminated the reference footnotes. (For those that want to read further, I have listed some of the more interesting references in the *Bibliography* section.)

One thing became quite clear in doing the research for this book: Not enough research has been done! There are many, many unanswered questions. If I had waited for the research to be done professionally, or waited until I could have completed it myself, this book may never have appeared! So in this edition a lot of those unanswered questions will have to remain unanswered. But I'm sure that there will be future editions of this book as hop research continues and new varieties appear.

I hope you'll get a lot of enjoyment out of *Using Hops* and most importantly that we'll both be making better, more consistent beers. With that thought in mind, I'll raise an imaginary glass to you and say "Cheers!"

Mark Garetz, Winter 1993/1994

Chapter 1 - Hop History

No one is quite sure when hops were first used in beer, but suffice it to say that it was a long time ago. One commonly sees references to the effect that hops first gained widespread acceptance in Europe in the 16th century, some say as late as 1650 (which is the 17th century). These may be referring to England, but certainly not to Europe. In fact, there is evidence that hops were used in England much earlier, as far back as the 11th century.

The first written evidence of the cultivation of hops is from the Hallertau district in Germany (still a major hop producing region) and dates from 736 AD. In any case, the famous Bavarian Beer Purity Law, the Reinheitsgebot, *legislates* the requirement for hops in beer, and that is from 1516 (early 16th century). One can only assume that the use of hops in beer was a well accepted and widespread practice for it to be passed into law.

Hop Growing Regions

Hops are grown in virtually every part of the world where beer is produced. Hops appear to have originated as a species in Asia and then spread eastward to North America and westward to Europe. Hop pollen has been discovered in archaeological digs in England dating as far back as 3000 BC. In any case, hops are considered indigenous to Middle Europe, England, North America and

Scene in a typical hop yard. Photo courtesy of Dave Wills.

Asia, with each area having evolved its own unique set of species.

The area where the hops are grown can make a significant difference in the characteristics of the hop. Some contend that hops indigenous to one region of the world cannot be simply transplanted to another and expect all of the hop's virtues to be identical, or even close. Others disagree with this statement and attribute the perceived differences to other factors such as different drying methods and changes in long ocean journeys. Whatever the truth is, there is still a lot of market value associated with the region in which the hop is grown, and is why many hops are named after the region where they were indigenous. The hops that have evolved in a particular area are called "land race" varieties (not because they race over the land, but because they are the "race" (breed) that grows in this particular land).

In Germany, three areas are of importance: The aforementioned Hallertau district in southern Germany (Bavaria), the region around Lake Constance called Tettnang (located further south and west) and the area called Spalt. We'll discuss the subject of "noble" hops later, but of the four noble hops in the world, one is from each of these areas.

In the Czech Republic (formerly Czechoslovakia) near the town of Zatec, another noble hop is grown. It is called Saaz after the original (and German) name of the town. Hops are also grown in Yugoslavia (Slovenia), and the Lubelski/Lublin varieties from Poland are considered as good as those from Czechoslovakia.

In England, hops have long been grown in the area of Kent, with East Kent being preferred. The hops from these areas are highly prized, but they are not considered noble by the trade. Hops went with the English settlers to Australia, New Zealand, South Africa and to the U.S.

Hops in the U.S. were originally grown in New York, then Michigan, and then Northern and Central California. The first hops grown here commercially were from English stock, but eventually became crossbred with indigenous American varieties. There is virtually no hop production in any of these areas now, with all U.S. production in the Pacific Northwest. The Yakima Valley in Washington is the largest growing area, followed by Oregon and Idaho. In Europe, the "Americans" were considered inferior because of their "wild" aroma. But with breeding and the move of hops from New York to California, hops from America were considered to be as good as English or European hops. One English author wrote in 1891, "American hops were formerly very inferior, and especially coarse in flavour. Cultivation and improvement in the varieties grown have, however, done great things, and some samples from the other side of the Atlantic are, in the present day, everything that could be desired."

Old vs. Modern Hops

Many of the "old" hop varieties survive today. Those that have survived have done so mainly because the hops' brewing qualities are highly prized. But, as was mentioned earlier, most of these land race varieties are only successful when grown in the area where they were first cultivated. The costs associated with transporting these hops over long distances, and the deterioration that takes place during the transport, as well as problems with foreign currency exchange (in olden times) led hop growers to attempt to select new varieties that performed well when grown closer to home. In addition, there have always been efforts to improve crop yields, and recently to select varieties more resistant to disease and pests.

Throughout the years, this work has continually provided new varieties of hops to the market. Even some of the old "standbys" such as East Kent Goldings were originally the result of selection done (by Mr. Golding) in the previous centuries.

Recently, hop breeding has focused on three areas: Duplicating noble hop characteristics in hops grown in different regions (such as here in the U.S.), increasing the disease resistance and/or improving the yield of the noble and other highly prized hops, and developing hops that are high in alpha acid content while having good storage properties. The first of these is really no different than historical breeding programs, but now we have better analysis tools to tell us how close we're getting. Developing disease resistance is essential because each year more and more of the Hallertauer Mittelfrüh (the noble Hallertau hop) is lost to verticillium wilt, and once that disease is established in a growing region, it cannot be eradicated.

The last area of research, breeding varieties high in alpha acid content, is fairly new. Alpha acids are that part of the hop that makes the beer bitter (much more on this later). There are many new varieties on the market that have two to five times the amount of alpha acids compared to aroma hops, and even two times the amount in traditional bittering hops. These hops are called *high alpha* or *super alpha* hops.

The good news for the brewer is that there are now a multitude of hops to choose from on the market. As craft brewers become more of a market force, we are increasingly able to get high quality traditional hops that were previously only available to large brewers. They are still expensive and always in tight supply, but they are available and that couldn't be said a few years ago! We can also benefit from the research that has produced (and will continue to produce) successful domestic versions of the traditional hops. And although the economic advantages of the high alpha hops don't make that much difference to the typical craft brewer, we now have many more bittering hops to choose from as a result.

Hop Levels in Beer - Then vs. Now

Hops became popular in beer because of their flavor, but also because they have a preservative quality. Before our modern sanitation techniques and sterile filtration came about (and indeed before brewers even knew what yeasts and bacteria were), hops were used at a much higher level than today because more preservative power was needed. For ales made to drink immediately, the hopping rate was not much different than a microbrewed or homebrewed ale would have today. But if the beer needed to be stored for long periods before consumption (called stock or store ales) then the hopping rates would be increased considerably. If the beer had to be shipped, such as India Pale Ale, it was common for these beers to be made twice as bitter as "home" ales.

Chapter 2 - Hops in Beer, A Brief Introduction

Later on in the book, we're going to go into great detail about how hops are used in beer. But I thought it would be a good idea to go over the basics and define some terms so we won't have to stop every few sentences later on in the book to explain something. This will cause some of the information to be repeated, but it will make the later chapters easier to read.

Hops are used to provide three effects in finished beer that we can taste or smell, and to provide a preservative effect. When we add hops to beer, we do so in a manner to create the sensory effects we desire, and the preservative effects come along for free. Therefore, we will not spend too much time talking about these preservative effects, other than to mention they're an added benefit.

First, a little controversy! Many authors have described the bitter flavor imparted to beer by hops simply as the "hop flavor". Well I'll agree that "bitter" is a flavor sensation, but it is certainly not the *only* flavor that hops have! When I talk about a beer's "flavor", the last thing I think about is how bitter it is. I don't even think about bitterness when the term "hop flavor" comes up in conversation. Maybe it's just me. But when I hear the term "hop flavor" I think about the wonderful tastes the hop imparts *in addition to* the bitterness. These tastes come from late additions of hops or from dry hopping (described later) and are caused by the hop oils (which have nothing to do with bitterness). These also impart a hop aroma to the beer. To try and come up with terms to describe these effects (and not get you completely confused if you read something else), I have defined three ways that hops impart a sensory effect to beer. Bittering, Hop Character and Hop Aroma. Notice that the word flavor is not used, because I think these sensory effects are all flavors or contribute to them.

Bittering

We all know that beer is bitter. Most of this bitterness is provided by the hops. (Some bitterness can be provided by highly roasted grains, but the hops usually provide the bulk of the bitterness.)

The compounds in the hops that are responsible for the bitterness are known as the *alpha acids*. Note that the term is plural because there are actually many separate compounds that make up the alpha acids. Three of these are the most important, and they are *humulone*, *cohumulone* and *adhumulone*. All three of these compounds are bitter, and all three occur in varying proportions depending on the hop variety. It is believed that hops high in cohumulone have a harsher bitter character than hops with low cohumulone levels.

Hops also contain a second group of acids known as the *beta acids*. The beta acids are not bitter, and are generally ignored by brewers when we consider a hop's bittering potential. (They have other significance, but we'll get into that later in the book).

Back to the alpha acids. Although the alpha acids are bitter, they are not very soluble in wort, at least at lower temperatures and normal wort pH values. When we boil the wort (which is when bittering hops are added), a respectable amount of alpha acids can go into solution, but when the wort is cooled back down to pitching or fermenting temperatures, the alpha acids would all drop out of solution and the resulting beer would no longer be bitter.

Fortunately for us, as the alpha acids are boiled they go through a chemical change known as *isomerization*, which is a fancy word that means that the atoms in the molecule are rearranged, but none are lost. *Isomerized alpha acids*, commonly referred to as *iso-alpha acids*, are quite soluble in wort, so the beer stays bitter. We call the process of boiling the hops to impart a bitter flavor to the beer either *kettle hopping* or *bitter hopping*. The hops used for the purpose are called *kettle hops*, *bitter hops* or *bittering hops*.

Many brewers and homebrewers believe that it takes a really long time to get the alpha acids out of the hops and into solution, and that isomerization of the alpha acids happens fairly quickly. In fact, just the opposite is true. When hops are added to boiling wort, the alpha acids go into solution fairly quickly. The reason we have to boil the hops for long periods is because the isomerization takes a long time. The accompanying chart shows the concentration of alpha acids and iso-alpha acids in wort vs. boiling time.

Many homebrewers also believe that this is all that goes on in the bittering process - once you have the alpha acids in the wort and have isomerized them, they stay there. This is also not true. In fact, only around 20% of the alpha acids added to the wort in the hops make it as iso-alpha acids into the finished beer. Losses occur at many stages along the way, but the important ones are: inefficiency of the isomerization, loss on cooling of the wort (some are precipitated out and some stick to the break material), loss during fermentation and loss during filtering or other beer processing (which is not an issue for most homebrewers).

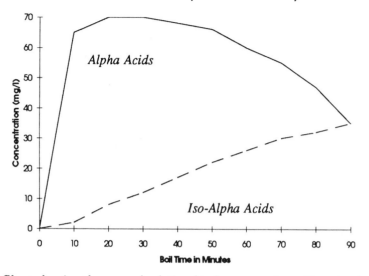

Chart showing the general relationship between apha acids going into solution and their isomerization as the boil progresses.

We talk about the efficiency of the whole process as the *percent utilization* as referenced to the amount of alpha acids we put in the beer to start with. So if we get 20% utilization, it means that only 20% of the alpha acids we added to the beer showed up in the bottle as iso-alpha acids. It is important to realize that we are talking about the amount of alpha acids put into the boiling wort compared to the amount of iso-alpha acids in the finished ready-to-drink beer. It does *not* refer to the simple efficiency of the wort boiling and isomerization process, and this is another common misconception homebrewers have when they talk about "utilization". If we *do* want to talk about the efficiency of the boiling process, we should refer to it as *kettle utilization* or *boil utilization* to make sure that we don't get confused. Later on, we'll present ways to calculate the amount of utilization that you will get, depending on the variables in your brewing practices. When we get there, we're going to have you factor in some post-boil corrections, based on your yeast, wort gravity etc. Just remember that we're going to try and figure the total utilization, not simply the kettle utilization.

There is a commonly accepted way of expressing just how bitter a beer actually is. Beer bitterness is expressed as *IBUs* which stands for International Bittering Units. The "international" comes from the fact that the U.S. and European brewing communities agreed on a standard unit and method of measurement. The IBU is roughly equivalent to the number of milligrams of iso-alpha acids in each liter of beer. The homebrewing community has other ways of attempting to express bittering units, and we'll discuss those later.

In summary, hops contain alpha acids, and these alpha acids are primarily responsible for bittering the beer. In order for the alpha acids to get into solution, they need to be isomerized, and this is accomplished by boiling the hops. We call this process kettle hopping or bitter hopping. The longer the boil time, the more the alpha acids are isomerized. Once the wort starts to cool, iso-alpha acids begin to be lost, and this loss continues throughout the brewing process. The final amount of iso-alpha acids in the beer vs. the amount of alpha acids we put in is known as the percent utilization, or simply as the utilization. We talk about the bitterness of the finished beer in IBUs.

Hop Character

In addition to alpha acids, hops also contain essential oils. These *hop oils* are responsible for the hop aroma that we smell in fresh hops. The oils impart a special flavor to the beer called the *hop character*. There is some aroma or *hop nose* associated with this flavor, but it is a completely different aroma than you get from fresh hops.

Hop oils are very volatile, meaning they evaporate

quickly. When the hops are boiled, most of the essential oils are lost in just a few minutes. If we want to retain some of the hop oils in the beer to give the beer some hop character, we need to add the hops very near the end of the boil (or even just after it). Even so, a lot of the hop oil components vanish almost instantly, and those that are left are changed due to the heat of the boil. This causes the flavor and aroma to be different than the aroma of fresh hops. Still, hop character is desirable in many beer styles.

The process of adding hops late in the boil to impart a hop character to the beer is called *late hopping, late kettle hopping* or *finish hopping*. The hops we use for this are generally called *aroma hops*, although occasionally you will see the term *late kettle hops* used. With very few exceptions, the choice of hops used to impart hop character to the beer is much more important than the choice of bittering hops. This is mainly because the differences in hop aroma and the resulting hop character are much easier to distinguish than the differences in the bitter characters.

The longer the hops are in the boiling wort, the less hop character they will impart, and the further that character will be from the aroma of fresh hops. As a practical limit, most late hop additions are confined to 15 minutes before the end of the boil, or less. It is not uncommon for several late hop additions to be made, for example one at 10 minutes before end-of-boil, another at 5 minutes and another right as the heat is turned off, allowing the hops to steep as the wort cools. Since the contact time with boiling wort is so short, little or none of the alpha acids have a chance to become isomerized, so these late hop additions have a minimal impact on the beer's actual bitterness.

There is no practical way for me to describe the taste of hop character to you. But beyond giving a unique flavor to the beer, it also has two other effects: it tends to make a beer's bitterness a little more pronounced, and it tends to enhance the body or mouthfeel of the beer.

Another way to get hop character in the beer is with a device known as a *hop back* (and sometimes as a *hop jack*). The hop back has been used in breweries for many centuries, but mainly as a strainer to hold back the spent hops from the wort as it went on to the coolers (you can see where the term hop back came from, because it held the hops back). It was either a metal plate with holes cut in it to act like a sieve, or a piece of cloth such as cheesecloth. It not only caught the spent hops, but also acted as filter for the hot break or trub. Somewhere along the line, brewers discovered that if they put fresh hops onto the hop back before they started running the wort through it, that it added hop character to the beer, but in slightly different ways than with simple late hop additions. The hop nose was more like (but not exactly like) that of fresh hops. These days, hop backs are mainly employed for their ability to impart hop character to the beer, and not as a filter. The hop back is now enclosed and keeps even more of the hop oils in the beer.

In summary, hop character is imparted to beer by the addition of hops very late in the boil, and sometimes after the boil by steeping the hops as the wort cools, and/or in a hop back. The effect is caused by the hop oils contained in the hops, and not from the alpha acids. Since the contact time with boiling wort is so short, the alpha acids don't get a chance to isomerize, so late hopping has very little, if any, effect on a beer's bitterness. It does however, increase the perception of a beer's bitterness, as well as its mouthfeel or body. There is a certain amount of hop aroma (or hop nose) associated with late hopping, but it is entirely different than that of fresh hops, due to the fact that certain of the oil compounds are lost, and those that remain are changed by the heat of the wort.

Hop Aroma

As was described above, the hop aroma imparted to a beer is caused by the hop oils. There is nothing quite like the aroma of fresh hops, and brewers throughout the centuries have tried to get that aroma in their beers. Adding hops near the end of the kettle boil does give the beer a hop aroma, but it is different than a fresh hop aroma. Use of the hop back gets the aroma a little closer, but it is still quite different.

To get the real aroma of fresh hops in the beer, brewers discovered that they needed to add hops very late in the process indeed. In the days when beer was served only from the cask, hops were added directly to the cask as the beer was racked into it, and the cask sealed. The beer was then shipped to the local pub and allowed to "come into condition" for a period of a week or two and then served. Because the hops had been added to beer that was at cellar temperatures (around 55°F) the hop oils did not undergo changes from the heat as they did in late hopping. And since the cask was sealed, there was no place for the volatile hop oils to evaporate to. So the beer had a fresh hop aroma imparted to it! This process is known as *dry hopping*, but it also used to be called *raw hopping*. No one seems to know why it was called "dry" hopping - hops are added "dry" at all stages of the process, at least these days. And that may account for it because it was once quite common to put the wet hops from the boil of the "first runnings" in with the boil of the second runnings (along with more fresh hops) and similarly to put the resulting spent hops in with the third runnings. These three worts were then combined to make the final beer. (For those of you that aren't all-grain brewers, water is run through the grain after its starches have been converted to sugars to extract the sugars from the grain. It can be done in one continuous process, and that's usually the way it is done today. But many years ago it was common to run water through the grain in three separate batches, which were boiled separately and then combined to be fermented. Presumably this was done because of limitations in the size of the boiling kettle. But we digress.)

In England (and in a few places in Canada and the U.S.) there is a move back to "real ales" that are cask conditioned and dry hopped in the traditional manner (thanks mainly to the efforts of CAMRA, the Campaign for Real Ale). Homebrewers usually dry hop by putting the hops in the secondary fermenter or into the serving kegs for those of us that use kegging systems.

As with late hopping, dry hopping adds no bitterness to the beer, but it can increase the beer's perceived bitterness. It can also increase the beer's mouthfeel. It should also be mentioned that a beer that has been dry hopped is also usually late hopped as well.

The choice of hops used for dry hopping is even more important than for late hopping. This is because we are trying to get all the aroma to come through in the finished beer. If there are any aroma defects in the hops, they will be noticeable in the finished beer. As with late hopping, generally only aroma hops are used for dry hopping, and of these, only the finest examples.

In summary, fresh hop aroma is imparted to beer by adding hops very late in the brewing process (as late as possible) in a process known as dry hopping. The hop aroma comes from the hop oils, and since dry hopping is a low temperature process, the hop aroma is not changed due to heat, as is the case in late hopping. As in late hopping, a beer's perceived bitterness can be increased with dry hopping, although the beer's actual bitterness is not affected.

Chapter 3 - The Hop Plant

This chapter will give you a brief overview of the hop plant itself. We're not going to spend a lot of time in this chapter, mainly because it doesn't really matter that much in brewing if you know your bracts from your bracteoles. But you should have a basic understanding of the hop plant's parts, and that's what this chapter is all about.

The Hop Plant in General

Hops are one of the two members of the plant family *Cannabinacae*, of which the only other member is *Cannabis* (of which *marijuana* is the most well known). There are chemical similarities between the two plants, but the resins are distinctly different. (In the '60s, grafts were attempted between marijuana and hops in attempt to produce a legal version of marijuana, but the resins didn't cross the graft.) Some will tell you that highly hopped beer has an extra "kick" due to the hops, but I treat these comments as wishful thinking. Hops have been used as a soporific (sleep inducer) in hop pillows and host of other "herbal" remedies, so I'll leave it to you to decide if hops have any powers beyond the magic they already perform in beer.

There are only two recognized species of hops: *Humulus lupulus* and *Humulus japonicus*. *Humulus japonicus* is an annual ornamental vine and has virtually no resins, so it has no value to us in brewing. If you haven't figured it out by now, *Humulus lupulus* is the hop we use in beer.

The hop plant is a vine, and will naturally climb on anything it finds. In commercial hop yards, the hop vine is trained up long strings of twine between 18-20 feet high. The twine is suspended from a wirework held up by poles and there are many patterns of wirework used.

The alpha acid and beta acids are part of the resin produced by the hop plant. The resin is produced along with the hop oils in microscopic yellow glands known as the *lupulin glands*. The lupulin glands only occur in significant quantities in female hop plants, so male hop plants are not used in brewing. (Male hop flowers have from 10-15 glands each, while the female flowers have greater than 10,000!)

No book on hops would be complete without some obligatory pictures of hop vines growing up their trellises and line drawings of hop plant parts. This book will not be the exception!

The Hop Vine

The plant itself consists of 4 major components: The *crown* which consists of the roots and rhizomes, the central stem known as the bine or vine, the leaves and the flowers or hop cones. The flowers are the only part of the plant that we put in beer (intentionally, anyway), so they get their own section later.

The *rhizome* of the hop plant is an underground stem that stays in the ground from year-to-year and is the real perennial part of the plant. From the rhizome the roots grow downwards and hop shoots will sprout in the spring. Each one of these shoots can become a bine. In practice, only the strongest few shoots will be left to grow so as to concentrate all of the plant's energy into the chosen bines.

Young hop vines in a hop yard. Photo by Ulrich Gampert.

Once the strongest bines have been selected, the others are trimmed away. When the bine is a few feet long, it is trained up a twine that has been anchored near the plant's base. The bine will twist its way up the twine until it reaches the top where it will flop over.

The hop leaves grow out from the bine in pairs. Although whole hops are commonly referred to by many brewers and authors as "leaf hops", this is a misnomer. Trust me, you don't want to brew with the leaves!

The hop plant is harvested by cutting the bine at the base and the twine at the top. The whole vine is then put on a truck and taken indoors where it is processed in a "picker" that removes the cones from the plant. The process is not perfect and whole hops typically contain some bine and leaf pieces, but not more than 2%.

As was mentioned earlier, the rhizome stays in the ground until the next season. If you want to try your hand at growing your own hops, see the chapter on the subject later in the book.

The Hop Cone

The hop *cone* or *flower* is the part of the hop plant we care about when we get to the brewhouse. The technical term for the cone is the *strobilus* or *strobile*, but I'll just call it the cone or flower, if that's OK with you. The hop cone of the female hop plant consists of 5 major components:

The central stem that holds the cone together is known as the *strig*. Growing off the strig are the *bracts* and the *bracteoles*. They look about the same, little pear-shaped green petals, but the bract (technically known as the *stipular bract*) has no brewing goodies. The bracteole though, has the lupulin glands and the seeds, if there are any. Nearly all of the domestic US hops are grown seedless. Most of the traditional English hops such as Fuggle and East Kent Goldings have seeds, but the trend in the UK today is to grow all varieties seedless. It will take some time before all the hops from the UK are seedless (if ever), so expect to see seeds if you get imported UK hops.

The Lupulin Glands

At the base of the bracteole is the part we really care about: the lupulin glands. The tiny, yellow lupulin glands are filled with resinous material, and this material contains the alpha and beta acids and the hop oils. Because the lupulin glands are yellow, tiny and easily dislodged, they seem like pollen, but they are not. In olden times, this yellow dust was called "condition" and I'm not sure how that term relates to "conditioning the beer" which we associate with the beer becoming carbonated. Since early "cask conditioned" ales were also dry hopped, the term "cask conditioning" may come from the fact that "condition" was added as the cask was bunged.

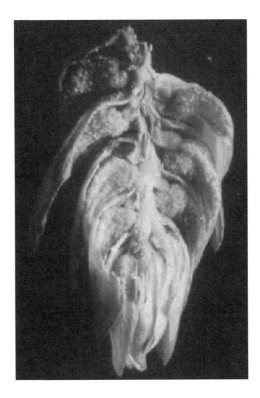

Cutaway view of hop cone showing the bracts, bracteoles, strig, seeds and you can even see the mass of lupulin glands. Photo courtesy of Dave Wills.

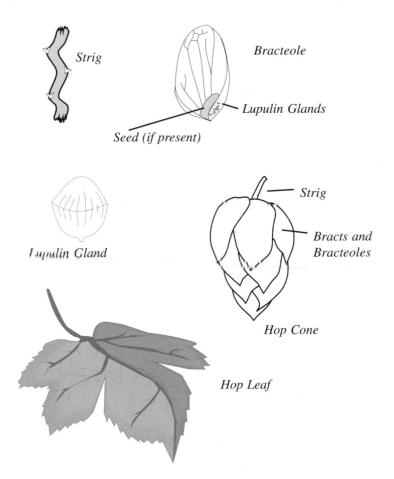

Diagrams of a hop strig, bracteole, lupulin gland, hop leaf and a whole hop cone. These are not to scale to one another and of course are highly stylized.

Chapter 4 - Hop Varieties

Although there is only one hop species (*Humulus lupulus*) that is useful for brewing, there are many varieties (technically known as *cultivars*) in that species. Each of these varieties has different brewing, growing and storage characteristics. Almost all of the hop varieties in use today are the result of hop breeding by hop researchers and not mother nature. In the early days, this consisted of selecting those plants that were desirable, but now more sophisticated techniques are used to create new varieties. In this chapter we'll detail the important characteristics of the popular hop varieties.

Hop Names

In order to keep track of all these hop varieties, common names are associated with specific varieties. Some of these names are traditional, and newer US hop varieties have their names chosen and sanctioned by a group consisting of the USDA and hop research centers in Washington, Oregon and Idaho. The newer names are usually chosen by the person responsible for breeding the original cultivar, and sometimes by the hop brokers that have invested in growing the first commercial-scale plots. The choice of names is fairly arbitrary; sometimes they are named after a place (like Mt. Hood, Cascade or Willamette) and sometimes just a nice-sounding word (like Centennial,

Crystal or Liberty). Traditional European hop names often were named after the person or institution that bred or selected them, and also often have the place where they are grown included in the name. Note that this is different than US hops named after places which generally have little to do with the area where they are grown.

Decoding European Hop Names

As was mentioned earlier, European (mainly German) hops usually have the growing region as part of the hop's name. The primary reason for this is that most of the important European varieties only produce the desired brewing qualities when grown in a specific region. Through many years of natural selection, varieties that are indigenous to the growing area have emerged, and these are called land races. These indigenous varieties are typically named for the place where they emerged, mainly because only one variety was grown there, so there was no need to be more specific. Some of these varieties are still grown in their place of origin and some are not.

European hops may have the same variety name as the place where they originated. But because these hops may no longer be grown in the place after which they are named, the place where they are *now* being grown is attached to the hop name as an adjective. Here's an example: A common hop from Germany is the variety called *Hersbrucker*. It originated in the *Hersbruck* region. It is called a Hersbruck<u>er</u> because it came from Hersbruck. Think about it this way: If you came from New York, we could call you a New York<u>er</u>. The "er" is always part of the variety name. If this hop was grown in the Hersbruck region, this hop would be called a *Hersbruck Hersbrucker*. But most of the Hersbrucker grown today is actually grown in the Hallertau region. Hersbrucker grown in the Hallertau region would be called *Hallertau Hersbrucker*.

This gets confusing because there is also a *Hallertauer* variety. When it is grown in the Hallertau, it is called *Hallertau Hallertauer*. Now I'm going to throw one more curve at you: The most prized hop in the world is the noble hop *Hallertauer Mittelfrüh*. "Now wait a minute!" I hear you say, "I thought I was just getting this straight, and here's a hop name with an "er" on the first word." Well right you are, it doesn't appear to be "correct". Well that's because the real name for this hop is *Hallertau Hallertauer Mittelfrüh*. Mittelfrüh means "middle-early" and has to do with the fact that this hop matured "middle-early" in the growing season. Hallertauers that matured at different times just weren't the same. So "Hallertauer Mittelfrüh" is a sub-variety of Hallertauer. To shorten the name up, most people leave off the first Hallertau since all Hallertauer Mittelfrüh was assumed to be grown in the Hallertau.

Let's recap how German hop names are put together: The first word is the place where this actual hop is grown. It does not have an "er" on it. The second word is the variety name. If the variety was named after a place, it has "er" tacked on the end. Sometimes there is a third word that can describe a sub-variety, in which case the first word (where its now grown) is sometimes dropped. Examples are Hallertauer Mittelfrüh and Hallertauer Tradition.

Now if someone is selling something they simply call "Hallertau" your first question should be "Hallertau what?" Usually this will be Hallertauer grown here in the US. Don't assume that just because the word Hallertau is used that the hop was grown in Germany. And if it is from Germany, you now know that "Hallertau" only tells you where the hop was grown, not which variety (lots of different varieties are grown in the Hallertau). We'll get more into depth on this subject in the chapter on buying hops. Lastly, don't make the assumption that just because a hop is grown in the Hallertau that it is an aroma hop. Northern Brewer is a bittering hop and is grown quite extensively in the Hallertau.

But not all German hops (especially the new ones) are named after a place. But since so much importance is placed on the famous German hop regions, if the hop was grown in one of these regions, you will see the name of the region as the first word in the hop name. But the second word may not have an "er" on the end. Perle was developed in Germany, and if it was grown in the Hallertau it would be sold as Hallertau Perle.

In Britain, hops are not named after the places where they were grown, but sometimes are named after the person who selected the hop. *Goldings* is named after Mr. Golding and *Fuggle* is named after Mr. Fuggle. A lot of the newer English varieties start with the word *Wye* because they were developed at Wye University's hop research department. Examples are *Wye Target*, *Wye Northdown* and *Wye Challenger* (sometimes the *Wye* is dropped). Sometimes they add the place as an adjective on the front of the hop name just like the German varieties. Goldings is an example, grown most favorably in the east part of Kent, and therefore sold as *East Kent Goldings*. And sometimes there are British hop names that are arbitrary like the US hop names. *Northern Brewer* and *Brewer's Gold* are two examples.

Other European hops don't follow any rules concerning their names. *Saaz* (or, more correctly, *Saazer*) is named for the town near which it grows in Czechoslovakia (the town is now called Zatec and Czechoslovakia now the Czech Republic). When marketed outside of Czechoslovakia, it is usually called *Czech Saaz* to distinguish it from the Saazer variety grown elsewhere. Slovenia (which used to be part of Yugoslavia) grows fine hops, and they have "Styrian" on the front of the hop name. It is curious the Styria is not in Slovenia, but in Austria. I have not been able to determine why hops from Slovenia are called "Styrian" but it is probably because it sounded better and it may be related to the old Austro-Hungarian Empire. This brings up an interesting point about the "market value" of the names of Slovenian hops: *Styrian Goldings* is indeed grown in Slovenia, but it is not a Goldings variety. It is really Fuggle, but the hop merchants there called it Goldings because they thought they could get more money for them (since Goldings was more highly thought of than Fuggle). To this day, the strategy still works! (Another theory is that the hop rootstocks were imported from England as "Fuggles Golding", for the exact same marketing reasons, so the blame may lie at the hands of the English hop exporters and not the Slovenian hop merchants.)

The "Noble" Hops

We've mentioned noble hops before, but now it's time to take a closer look. There are four recognized noble hops: Hallertauer Mittelfrüh, Tettnang Tettnanger, Czech Saaz and Spalt Spalter. All four are "aroma" hops, but the finest lagers use them for bittering as well. Where the term "noble" comes from is anybody's guess, but it is apparent that these hops achieved "nobility" because they were prized above all others by European brewers. The brewing properties of the noble hops are unique from all other hops, and also unique from each other. It is very hard to describe what the "noble hop aroma" is like, but it is certainly "mellow" compared to other hops.

To be considered a true noble hop (by the hop trade anyway), they must be grown in the correct region. That is why so much emphasis is placed on the growing regions in Germany (and the town of Saaz used to be in Germany). Tettnanger grown anywhere outside of the Tettnang region is not a true noble hop. It may have all the same brewing characteristics, but it shouldn't command a noble hop price. History has shown that if you take a noble hop and try and grow it somewhere else, it may lose some of its noble character, and that is also why the growing region is so important (in addition to the "marketing" value).

Before the days of sensitive laboratory equipment and analysis, no one knew what made a noble hop "noble". Brewers and growers relied on another sensitive instrument, their noses! But now we can analyze the hops to find out what makes them noble. This is going to get a little technical, but here's what we know that noble hops have in common, and how they differ from other hops: An alpha/beta ratio of about 1:1, relatively low alphas and betas (2 to 5%), low cohumulone content, low myrcene in the hop oil (typically below 50%), high humulene in the oil, a ratio of humulene to caryophyllene above 3, and relatively poor storage characteristics (meaning the hops are more naturally prone to oxidation than others).

Of the hops around today, the four noble varieties meet all these criteria. A variety of Saazer grown in Poland and called *Lubelski* (or sometimes *Lublin*) also meets the criteria and is sometimes considered a proper noble hop (but it is not widely available). English Fuggle and Goldings come close, and some call them noble as well, but mainly those who are selling them. Hallertauer Mittelfrüh is declining in production due to its susceptibility to verticillium wilt, and the Germans are trying to substitute other varieties and now call them noble as well. Hersbrucker was the most common of these, and while it has a fine aroma and is close to noble in character, it doesn't quite get noble status. The German hop breeders released Perle and it was supposed to be a replacement for Hallertauer Mittelfrüh. But Perle's alphas were too high, so brewers didn't accept it as noble (but it is well accepted as a bittering hop). Two new German hops, Spalter Select and Hallertauer Tradition are claimed to be noble in character, but time will tell if they are accepted or not.

US vs. European Grown

In the US, hop researchers have been trying to come up with a hop that duplicates the noble characteristics of Hallertauer Mittelfrüh, while being able to be grown successfully in the US. The first hop released from these efforts was *Mt. Hood*. The trial plots of this hop showed great promise, but commercial plantings didn't turn out quite as good. Nevertheless, Mt. Hood is a fine hop and is now well established with brewers here. (I should mention that the suspected reasons for the difference in the trial plots and the commercial plots was due to the lack of rain in the years of commercial growth vs. the trial years. 1993 had rain levels that were more normal, and the Mt. Hood from 1993 was much more "noble" than in previous years.) A few years later, *Liberty* was released and is very close to Hallertauer Mittelfrüh (closer than Mt. Hood). Recently, *Crystal* was released and also comes very close (it's a toss-up between Liberty and Crystal as to which one is the closest). These hops are all sisters, with Hallertauer Mittelfrüh as the female parent. They are all triploids (pronounced trih´-ployed) which means they have 30 chromosomes instead of the usual diploid (dih´-ployed) hops which have 20 chromosomes. Triploids are naturally seedless, but they can also be more disease resistant.

What about domestic Hallertauer? Sorry, but it doesn't grow the same in the US as it does in Germany, (it doesn't come out quite as noble and the yield is quite poor). If it did grow the same, there wouldn't have been all the effort behind the breeding of Mt. Hood, Liberty and Crystal. The same is true of Saazer and Spalter, and to a lesser extent Tettnanger. Breeding programs are under way now to come up with varieties that will duplicate Czech Saaz and Tettnang Tettnanger, and it will be a few more years until they are released.

In the meantime, imported Czech Saaz is available to homebrewers (Hallertauer Mittelfrüh *never* is and there is little doubt that this hop will soon be "history") and domestic Tettnanger isn't as far off the mark as domestic Hallertauer and Saazer. Spalt Spalter is also available from time-to-time and the newer Hallertauer Tradition and Spalter Select varieties should be fairly easy to obtain.

Individual Hop Varietal Characteristics

This section will list the most popular hop varieties and their characteristics. Some guidelines will be given as to their brewing characteristics and the styles for which they are most appropriate. I would like to have given a lot more information on the hops' brewing properties, but this data is hard to come by. Firstly, everyone's taste buds are different, and what I hate you may love. Secondly, it's hard to get two brewers to agree on how a hop affects a beer. Lastly, why worry? Don't be afraid to experiment. Beer styles are not fixed in stone (unless you're entering your beer in competition), but are constantly evolving. Home and microbrewers will be the ones to create new styles.

I would also like to have given more data on what hops are used by a particular brewery for a particular beer, the hopping schedules, etc. Where I know the beer is generally available nationally and has been in production unchanged for some time, I will supply some data. But beer recipes are subject to change, and most of the really interesting beers are only distributed in a small area. This means that not only is there a good chance that I've never heard of or tasted them, but if I gave the hop bill for that beer, it wouldn't mean much to readers outside that area. If you really want to know what hops are in a given beer, your best bet is to simply ask the brewer. Usually they will tell you all you need to know, and if they won't, well it means they probably wouldn't tell me either (or at least I couldn't print it!).

The hops in this section are organized into two categories: Bittering and aroma hops. Within each category, the hops are presented alphabetically for easy reference. Each hops' description starts with some general information about the variety, including a guide to pronunciation (but only for the weird names - I didn't feel I needed to tell you how to pronounce Liberty for example). It then lists some of the more important varietal characteristics such as alpha acids content, storageability, aroma perception and country of origin. This is followed by some general comments on the usage of the hop, and this includes appropriate beer styles and other comments related to how you might use the hop. Lastly I've included some data on which hops would be the best substitutes if the variety is unavailable.

Now the question arises about the actual usefulness of some of the hop compound data. Most hops you get will be rated for alpha acids content, and depending on the supplier, the hops may also be rated for oil content. But the other characteristics are never actually measured and given to the brewer the way the previous two are. So why list them? Firstly, it's kind of traditional. It is mainly used as a way to contrast one hop variety vs. another. Secondly, the compounds I've chosen to list are generally those that have a direct effect on the hop's brewing characteristics, and also those that are used to distinguish "noble hops" from others.

Using the Hop Compound Data

First the fine print: As you know, hops are a plant, and being a plant they are subject to the whims of mother nature. Therefore, we can talk about the amount of a certain hop compound for a given variety only as an average value, not an absolute number. The data below was compiled from a number of sources. Some listed average ranges for a value, and some are simply the average and presented as a single value. Please note the following: These are the typical values *at harvest*, and they will change as the hops age. Also, sometimes a hop will be out of range. For example, Cascade's average alpha acid range is listed as 5.5-7%. But this year (1993) one lot of Cascade had alphas at harvest of 7.4%.

Alpha Acids: This is the range of typical values at harvest for the total of all the alpha acids. It is listed as a percentage weight of the total hop weight (w/w). The alpha acids figure is used to determine the amount of bitterness in the final beer, and is the most important measure of the hop. Always use the value you get with hops, not the value in this book. And don't be too concerned if the value seems low or high compared to what's listed here.

Beta Acids: This is the range of typical values at harvest for the total of all of the beta acids. It is listed as a percentage weight of the total hop weight (w/w). This figure is mainly given for reference, and is not normally used in brewing.

Alpha/Beta Ratio: This is the average ratio of the alpha to beta acids, figured by dividing the alpha by the beta percentages. This figure is mainly provided as a reference and is not normally used in brewing. It is significant because ideally "noble" hops have an alpha/beta ratio very close to 1.

Cohumulone %: Cohumulone is one of the alpha acids, and this figure is either the range of typical values (or a single figure representing the simple average of the range) at harvest. It is a percentage of the total alpha acids. The percentage of cohumulone is considered by many hop researchers to be significant because of the theory that hops with a high percentage of cohumulone have a "harsh" bitterness. Certainly "noble" hops and most aroma hops have a much lower cohumulone level than most bittering hops. But some bittering hops that have relatively high cohumulone levels aren't noted for their harsh bitterness. Debate rages on among hop researchers on this issue, and nothing is conclusive. My guess is that cohumulone plays a role in harshness, but probably interacts in a yet-undiscovered way with some other hop or beer compound. Some also claim high cohumulone gives better utilization.

Total Oils: This is the range of typical values (or a single figure representing the simple average of the range) for the total of all hop oil compounds at harvest. It is listed as a percentage volume of oil in the total weight of the hops (v/w). Sometimes you also see this figure as ml/100 grams, and it is the same (2 ml/100 grams is equal to 2% v/w). While not a perfect indicator of the hoppiness potential of a given hop, we can use the total oil content as a guide to better control of aroma hopping rates, just like we use the alpha acids content to control bitter hopping rates.

Myrcene: Myrcene is one of the major hop oil constituents. This figure is listed as a percentage of the total oils (either a range of typical values or a single figure representing the average of the range). This figure is provided mainly for reference as it is not normally used in brewing. It is significant because ideally "noble" hops have a low percentage of myrcene, below 50%.

Humulene: Humulene is another of the major hop oil constituents. This figure is listed as a percentage of the total oils (either a range of typical values or a single figure representing the average of the range). This figure is provided mainly for reference as it is not normally used in brewing. It is significant because ideally "noble" hops have a high percentage of humulene. Humulene is also the precursor to most of the important hop oil oxidation products, so a hop with high humulene and relatively poor storage characteristics is more likely (but not guaranteed) to have better aroma characteristics with some aging, which causes these oxidation products to form.

Humulene/Caryophyllene Ratio: This is the average ratio of humulene to caryophyllene, figured by dividing the humulene by the caryophyllene percentages. Caryophyllene is another of the major oil constituents. This figure is mainly provided as a reference and is not normally used in brewing. It is significant because ideally "noble" hops have an humulene/caryophyllene ratio of at least 3, with 3.2 or higher preferred.

Aroma: This section contains some general comments on the hop's aroma profile.

Storage: Describes the storage characteristics of the variety in broad terms (like poor, good etc.) and also as a percentage of alpha acids lost after storage at room temperature (20°C) for 6 months. This figure is used later in the book to calculate alpha acids losses based on storage conditions and time. This figure is an average of the range for that variety.

It is also significant in that "noble" hops typically have poor storage characteristics (around 50% of the alphas lost).

Country of Origin: Lists the country where the hop is indigenous or was first bred. If the hop was bred in another country, but this description is about the hop when grown somewhere else, the original country and the country where we're talking about it being grown are both listed.

Usage: This section gives some general advice about what beer styles the variety would be appropriate for, and any other tidbits of information that are relevant to brewing with this hop. If I can, I sometimes list widely available commercial beers made with this hop.

Substitutes: This section lists possible substitutes for this variety. Sometimes a recipe will call for a specific variety and you may not be able to get that hop or want to brew with the closest available hop you have on hand. Generally, I have tried to list the most suitable substitutes first, and usually if it makes a big difference, I have commented on the order of suitability. The main exception is when I list Crystal, Liberty and Mt. Hood. This particular list of the three Hallertauer Mittelfrüh replacements is presented in alphabetical order. It's up to you to decide which of the three you like the best.

Bittering Hops

Brewer's Gold: Brewer's Gold was originally bred in England from a seedling of a wild Canadian hop. It is not widely used today, but it has an important role in hop history because it is the parent of quite a few of the more popular hops. It has a medium alpha acid levels and has been largely replaced by the high-alpha varieties. It is grown in England, Europe and to very a limited extent in the US. Do not confuse this hop with Goldings! They are not even similar.

Alpha Acids (typical): 5.5-8.5%

Beta Acids (typical): 2.9-4.5%

Alpha/Beta Ratio: 1.9

Cohumulone % (typical): 38%

Total Oil % (typical): 1.5%

Myrcene % (typical): 65%

Humulene % (typical): 12%

Humulene/Caryophyllene Ratio: 2.3

Aroma: Not highly regarded, but reasonably neutral in character.

Storage: Poor. 50% alpha acids lost after 6 months at 20°C.

Country of Origin: England

Usage: Appropriate for English Ales and can be used in heavier German-style lagers. In a pinch, it could be used for almost any style, but should be used to provide base bittering only (boil at least 60 minutes) and not for aroma hopping.

Substitutes: Northern Brewer, Galena or any other bittering hop to your liking.

Bullion: Bullion was bred in England as a seedling from the same Canadian wild hop as Brewer's Gold. I never associated the name Bullion with gold (as in gold bullion) until I knew this fact! It still remains in use today, but is being edged out in favor of the newer high alpha varieties that store better.

Alpha Acids (typical): 6.0-9.0%

Beta Acids (typical): 3.2-4.7%

Alpha/Beta Ratio: 1.9

Cohumulone % (typical): 36%

Total Oil % (typical): 3.2%

Myrcene % (typical): 64%

Humulene % (typical): 12%

Humulene/Caryophyllene Ratio: 1.5

Aroma: Not highly regarded, but reasonably neutral in character. High oil content means aroma may come through stronger if boil times are short or when used in a very light lager.

Storage: Poor. 50% alpha acids lost after 6 months at 20°C.

Country of Origin: England

Usage: Appropriate for English Ales and can be used in heavier German-style lagers. In a pinch, it could be used for almost any style, but should be used to provide base bittering only (boil at least 60 minutes) and not for aroma hopping. See note on high oil content under aroma heading.

Substitutes: Northern Brewer, Galena or any other bittering hop to your liking.

Centennial: Centennial is a medium-high to high alpha hop that was selected from a cross of Brewer's Gold and a male hop from the USDA breeding stock. It is fairly new, and is growing in popularity, especially amongst home and micro brewers. It has a very pleasant aroma that is reminiscent of Cascade. In fact, some call it a "Super Cascade" and even use it as an aroma hop. Before this hop got its official name, it was marketed as CFJ-90. It was named after the Washington State Centennial Celebration.

Alpha Acids (typical): 9.5-11.5%

Beta Acids (typical): 3.5-4.5%

Alpha/Beta Ratio: 2.6

Cohumulone % (typical): 29-30%

Total Oil % (typical): 1.5-2.3%

Myrcene % (typical): 45-55%

Humulene % (typical): 10-18%

Humulene/Caryophyllene Ratio: 2.2

Aroma: Medium with floral and citrus notes. Similar to Cascade.

Storage: Good. 37% alpha acids lost after 6 months at 20°C.

Country of Origin: USA, grown primarily in Washington.

Usage: Centennial is best used in American Pale Ales. It is great as a base bittering hop if the beer will be finished with Cascade as the two hops don't compete or clash, but rather compliment each other. Centennial has also been used with success in American-style wheat beers. Its bitter character is smooth, with no harsh or other distracting flavors.

Substitutes: Although not a bittering hop, Cascade is a good substitute for Centennial.

Chinook:
Chinook is a high alpha variety developed from a cross of an English Golding variety and a USDA male hop. Chinook is one of those hops that either you love or you hate. Even so, it remains quite popular and is widely grown. Personally, I don't like the bitter character of Chinook, but you'll have to decide for yourself. I highly respect the beers, brewing abilities and the palates of brewers that love Chinook. Beers that have a distinct Chinook signature have taken Gold Medals at the Great American Beer Festival. Some brewers even use Chinook as an aroma hop, even dry hopping with it, but those beers aren't for me. It just points up the fact that everybody's tastes are different. I recommend you try it and see if you like it.

Alpha Acids (typical): 12-14%

Beta Acids (typical): 3-4%

Alpha/Beta Ratio: 3.8

Cohumulone % (typical): 29-34%

Total Oil % (typical): 1.5-2.5%

Myrcene % (typical): 35-40%

Humulene % (typical): 20-25%

Humulene/Caryophyllene Ratio: 2.3

Aroma: Mild to Medium-Heavy, Spicy. Some brewers use Chinook as an aroma hop, but I can't personally recommend it. Your mileage may vary.

Storage: Good. 32% alpha acids lost after 6 months at 20°C.

Country of Origin: USA, grown primarily in Washington.

Usage: Chinook is used in everything from pale ales to lagers. In my opinion, it should be used only as a base bittering hop, and then only if the beer's bitterness will not be very high. Some brewers really like the aroma of Chinook, though.

Substitutes: Galena, Nugget or Cluster.

Cluster:
Cluster is the classic American bittering hop. For many years it was the only commercially grown hop in the US. No one is quite sure about Cluster's pedigree, but before the really high alpha varieties were introduced, Cluster was highly regarded for its high alpha content and excellent storage properties. Until a few years ago, Cluster was the most widely planted hop in the US, and had enjoyed that position for almost a century. Galena now occupies the number one slot, but Cluster is not far behind at number two. Cluster doesn't get used as much in homebrewing as it deserves. The fact that it is the second largest crop, testifies that commercial brewers think highly of it.

Alpha Acids (typical): 5.5-8.5%

Beta Acids (typical): 4.5-5.5%

Alpha/Beta Ratio: 1.3

Cohumulone % (typical): 36-42%

Total Oil % (typical): 0.4-0.8%

Myrcene % (typical): 45-55%

Humulene % (typical): 15-18%

Humulene/Caryophyllene Ratio: 2.5

Aroma: Medium and quite spicy. The low oil-to-alphas ratio means that very little if any of Cluster's aroma will be carried through into the beer from bittering additions. This is not a shortcoming, but helps keep Cluster one of the more neutral bittering hops.

Storage: Excellent. 17% alpha acids lost after 6 months at 20°C.

Country of Origin: USA

Usage: Cluster is the tried and true bittering hop. It has a very smooth, neutral bitterness with no objectionable characteristics. It is a great base bittering hop for any beer.

Substitutes: Galena or Chinook.

Eroica:
Eroica is a high alpha hop that is declining in popularity in favor of the better storing varieties. It was bred by open pollination of Brewer's Gold. It is still available to homebrewers, but since demand for this hop is dwindling, I would expect it to pretty much disappear over the next few years. It was named after the Beethoven symphony of the same name. Pronounced eh-roy´-ih-cah.

Alpha Acids (typical): 11-13%

Beta Acids (typical): 4-5%%

Alpha/Beta Ratio: 2.7

Cohumulone % (typical): 36-42%

Total Oil % (typical): 0.8-1.3%

Myrcene % (typical): 55-65%

Humulene % (typical): 0-1%

Humulene/Caryophyllene Ratio: 0.1

Aroma: Strong aroma when fresh, but will be almost non-existent with some aging due to the very low humulene content, which will also make the aroma quite "unbalanced" compared to other varieties.

Storage: Poor. 40% alpha acids lost after 6 months at 20°C.

Country of Origin: USA, grown primarily in Idaho.

Usage: Eroica should be used only as a base bittering hop and then only for full boils so the unbalanced aroma characteristics don't make it into the finished beer. My recommendation is not to get too attached to this hop, as it is going to get harder and harder to get.

Substitutes: Galena, Nugget, Chinook or Cluster.

Using Hops

Galena:
Galena is a high alpha hop that is the most widely planted in the US. Of the high alpha varieties, it has the most neutral bittering characteristics. Like Eroica, it too was bred from open pollination of Brewer's Gold. Galena is a very popular hop, and justifiably so. It has acceptable aroma profile and excellent storage properties. Pronounced: guh-lay´-nuh.

Alpha Acids (typical): 12-14%

Beta Acids (typical): 7-9%

Alpha/Beta Ratio: 1.6

Cohumulone % (typical): 38-42%

Total Oil % (typical): 0.9-1.2%

Myrcene % (typical): 55-60%

Humulene % (typical): 10-15%

Humulene/Caryophyllene Ratio: 3

Aroma: Medium with a pleasant hoppiness.

Storage: Excellent (actually, the best). 15% alpha acids lost after 6 months at 20°C.

Country of Origin: USA, grown primarily in Idaho.

Usage: If you could only stock one bittering hop, Galena would be the one. It is a great bittering hop and its neutral character makes it suitable for any style of beer. The fact that it stores well makes it that much more attractive.

Substitutes: Cluster, Nugget, Chinook.

Hallertau Northern Brewer: Northern Brewer was bred in England as a cross between a Goldings variety and Brewer's Gold. It ended up being much more popular in Germany, where it proved to be very resistant to the particular strain of verticillium wilt that was devastating the Hallertau. Northern Brewer is a medium alpha hop (by today's standards) and is still widely used. The most famous example is Anchor's Steam Beer, which uses Northern Brewer exclusively. Hallertau Northern brewer is far superior to the domestic. Little production, if any, remains in England.

Alpha Acids (typical): 7-10%

Beta Acids (typical): 3-5%

Alpha/Beta Ratio: 2

Cohumulone % (typical): 28-33%

Total Oil % (typical): 1.6-2.1%

Myrcene % (typical): 30-35%

Humulene % (typical): 25-30%

Humulene/Caryophyllene Ratio: 3.5

Aroma: Medium to strong, distinctive. Hallertau Northern Brewer is far superior to the domestic.

Storage: Excellent. 20% alpha acids lost after 6 months at 20°C.

Country of Origin: England, but now primarily grown in Germany.

Usage: Northern Brewer has a clean bitter character, but yet has a distinctive taste. Since this is the only hop used in the production of Anchor's famous Steam Beer, it is the obvious choice when making that style (also known as California Common Beer). But Northern Brewer is also useful in many other beers, especially German lagers and ales where it has been used extensively for quite some time. Hallertau Northern Brewer can be used as an aroma hop.

Substitutes: Domestic Northern Brewer or Perle.

Northern Brewer (domestic):Northern Brewer was bred in
England as a cross between a Goldings variety and Brewer's Gold.
Northern Brewer is a medium alpha hop (by today's standards) and is
still widely used. The most famous example is Anchor's Steam Beer,
which uses Northern Brewer exclusively. Little production, if any,
remains in England.

Alpha Acids (typical): 8-10%

Beta Acids (typical): 3-5%

Alpha/Beta Ratio: 2.2

Cohumulone % (typical): 20-30%

Total Oil % (typical): 1.5-2%

Myrcene % (typical): 50-60%

Humulene % (typical): 20-30%

Humulene/Caryophyllene Ratio: 3.5

Aroma: Medium to strong.

Storage: Good. 20% alpha acids lost after 6 months at 20°C.

Country of Origin: England, but now grown in the USA.

Usage: Northern Brewer has a clean bitter character, but yet
has a distinctive taste. Since this is the only hop used in the
production of Anchor's famous Steam Beer, it is the obvious
choice when making that style (also known as California
Common Beer). But Northern Brewer is also useful in many
other beers, especially German lagers and ales where it has
been used extensively for quite some time. Northern Brewer
can be used as an aroma hop, but I would recommend the
Hallertau Northern Brewer vs. the domestic for aroma
purposes.

Substitutes: Perle or Hallertau Northern Brewer.

Nugget:
Nugget is a high alpha hop that was bred from a cross between Brewer's Gold and a high alpha male hop that had good storage properties. Nugget is highly regarded by commercial brewers, but isn't very popular on the homebrewing scene, probably because of the over-abundance of high alpha varieties to choose from and the rather heavy, herbal aroma. However, Nugget is a fine general purpose bittering hop.

Alpha Acids (typical): 12-14%

Beta Acids (typical): 4-6%

Alpha/Beta Ratio: 2.7

Cohumulone % (typical): 24-30%

Total Oil % (typical): 1.7-2.3%

Myrcene % (typical): 51-59%

Humulene % (typical): 12-22%

Humulene/Caryophyllene Ratio: 2

Aroma: Heavy and herbal in character.

Storage: Good. 25% of alpha acids lost after 6 months at 20°C.

Country of Origin: USA, grown primarily in Oregon.

Usage: Nugget is a fine general purpose bittering hop. But the high oil content dictates use only for long boil times and not late additions, lest the aroma effects be carried into your beer (unless, of course, that's what you want). Probably not a good choice for light lagers.

Substitutes: Galena, Chinook, Cluster.

Using Hops

Perle:
Perle was originally bred in Germany as a disease-resistant alternative to Hallertauer Mittelfrüh, and great claims were made for the "nobleness" of this new hop. Use as a Hallertauer Mittelfrüh replacement never caught on, but Perle does enjoy good popularity as a medium alpha bittering hop. Some still classify it as an aroma hop. Imported Perle is not often available in the US, but it's not of much consequence since our domestic grown version is also excellent. Pronunciation of Perle is a tough one: Perle is the German word for "pearl" and some pronounce it as "pearl" would be pronounced in English. A lot of people pronounce it puhr´-lee (as in the pearly gates) but the correct, German pronunciation is pehr´-luh.

Alpha Acids (typical): 7-9.5%

Beta Acids (typical): 4-5%

Alpha/Beta Ratio: 1.8

Cohumulone % (typical): 27-32%

Total Oil % (typical): 0.7-0.9%

Myrcene % (typical): 45-55%

Humulene % (typical): 28-33%

Humulene/Caryophyllene Ratio: 2.8

Aroma: Pleasant and slightly spicy.

Storage: Excellent. 15% alpha acids lost after 6 months at 20°C.

Country of Origin: Germany, but widely grown (successfully) in the US.

Usage: Perle can be used successfully in almost any beer. It has an extremely clean, almost minty bitterness. I have used it in American Pale Ales and Porters with great success. It is very appropriate for German lagers and ales.

Substitutes: Northern Brewer or any good bittering hop such as Cluster or Galena.

Pride of Ringwood: Pride of Ringwood is the dominant

hop grown in Australia, accounting for more than 90% of the acreage. For a high alpha hop, it has decent aroma, but not much else to distinguish it over our domestic high alpha hops. Since it is a poor storing hop it is not very economical to import into this country. However, the area in Australia where it is grown is naturally free from pests and diseases that affect hops, making it easy to grow this hop organically. "Organic" Pride of Ringwood is being made available to microbrewers in this country wanting to produce a completely organic beer. As a consequence of this, it is also sometimes available to the homebrewing market.

Alpha Acids (typical): 9-11%

Beta Acids (typical): 5.3-6.5%

Alpha/Beta Ratio: 1.7

Cohumulone % (typical): 33%

Total Oil % (typical): 2%

Myrcene % (typical): 58%

Humulene % (typical): 1.5%

Humulene/Caryophyllene Ratio: 0.1

Aroma: Moderate. Not much other data available but the very low humulene content tells us that this hop's aroma will vanish quickly with any aging.

Storage: Poor. 50% alpha acids lost after 6 months at 20°C.

Country of Origin: Australia

Usage: If you're trying to duplicate an Australian beer, chances are good it was made with Pride of Ringwood. As mentioned above, if you want to make a truly organic beer, then Pride of Ringwood is your only hope of finding an organically grown hop (make sure the one you buy is certified as such). Unless you can certify that your grain is also organic, I wouldn't bother.

Substitutes: Galena, Cluster.

Using Hops

Super Styrians: Grown in Slovenia, the Super Styrians are
actually a group of four varieties, named Atlas, Apolon, Ahil and
Aurora. The first three were all seedlings of Brewer's Gold, and
the last was a seedling of Northern Brewer. These hops are not
marketed individually, and one is likely to get any of these
varieties or a mixture when buying "Super Styrians". They are
not commonly available in the US, but are presented here mainly
to point up the fact that they are quite different from Styrian
Goldings. Don't buy Super Styrians thinking you're getting a
better version of Styrian Goldings.

Alpha Acids (typical): 8-10%

Beta Acids (typical): 3.6-4.5%

Alpha/Beta Ratio: 2.2

Cohumulone % (typical): 25-30%

Total Oil % (typical): 0.8-1%

Myrcene % (typical): 58%

Humulene % (typical): 12%

Humulene/Caryophyllene Ratio: 2.5

Aroma: Information not available, but reported as "good".

Storage: Moderate. 27% alpha acids lost after 6 months at
20°C

Country of Origin: Slovenia (formerly Yugoslavia)

Usage: General purpose bittering. Given the relatively low
alpha acids content (compared to say Galena), the poor storage
qualities and the fact that you will pay more for this hop
because it's "imported", I would not bother with it.

Substitutes: Galena, Northern Brewer, Cluster.

Wye Target:
Wye Target is the most widely planted hop in England. Developed primarily as a high alpha hop, it is used by some brewers as an aroma hop as well. It does not seem to be available in the US, but I've included it here because many English beers are made with it, and brewers in the US are likely curious about this hop.

Alpha Acids (typical): 9.5-13%

Beta Acids (typical): 4.3-5.9%

Alpha/Beta Ratio: 2.2

Cohumulone % (typical): 35%

Total Oil % (typical): 1.4%

Myrcene % (typical): 63%

Humulene % (typical): 11%

Humulene/Caryophyllene Ratio: 2.4

Aroma: Some believe this is a bittering hop, others believe it can also be used as an aroma hop. At least one major brewery in the UK dry hops their cask conditioned ales with Target (but the export versions get East Kent Goldings).

Storage: Very poor. Exact % lost figures are not available.

Country of Origin: England

Usage: Widely used in all styles of English ales and lagers.

Substitutes: For bittering, any bitter hop you like. For aroma, there is no clear substitute. If you're making an English Ale, you can't go wrong with East Kent Goldings or Fuggle, but it won't be much like Target. You might try Northern Brewer or even Brewer's Gold. "By the numbers" they are very close, but that doesn't always mean anything.

Aroma Hops

B.C. Goldings: B.C. stands for British Columbia and B.C. Goldings is one of the Goldings variety grown in British Columbia. It doesn't quite measure up to the real thing, but is a useful substitute if no real East Kent Goldings are available. See East Kent Goldings for more details.

Cascade: Cascade is undoubtedly the most popular aroma hop with home and microbrewers. It is the signature hop in just about every American Pale Ale brewed on the West Coast. Cascade was bred from an open pollinated seedling of a cross of Fuggle and a Russian hop (Serebrianker), and has an aroma like no other. Cascade was very popular when it was introduced, then declined in popularity for a while, and is now popular once again. I know it is my favorite hop.

Alpha Acids (typical): 4.5-7%

Beta Acids (typical): 4.5-7%

Alpha/Beta Ratio: 1

Cohumulone % (typical): 33-40%

Total Oil % (typical): 0.8-1.5%

Myrcene % (typical): 45-60%

Humulene % (typical): 10-16%

Humulene/Caryophyllene Ratio: 4

Aroma: Pleasant, quite floral and somewhat spicy with definite citrus notes. Cascade's aroma is unique. Some brewers describe it as "grapefruity".

Storage: Poor. 50% alpha acids lost after 6 months at 20°C.

Cascade, continued.

Country of Origin: USA, grown in both Oregon and Washington.

Usage: Cascade is appropriate in American-style Pale Ales, where it is often used as both the bittering and aroma hop. Dry hopping with Cascade is very popular. As was mentioned above, Cascade is the signature hop in many commercial Pale Ales. In my opinion, Anchor's Liberty Ale is the finest example, using 100% Cascade, including dry hopping. Sierra Nevada's Pale Ale is also a fine example, with lots of Cascade in the finish. Even though Cascade is most often used in Pale Ales, feel free to create your own style and use Cascade. But be aware that the Cascade signature is unique and can be spotted in an instant by better beer judges and drinkers, so keep this in mind if you're trying to brew a beer "true-to-style" and it's not an American Ale. Cascade is also appropriate in barley wines, where again it is often dry hopped.

Substitutes: There really are none. The closest is Centennial. Substitution shouldn't really be much of a problem, unless you need to brew with hops on hand, because Cascade is always readily available.

Crystal: Crystal is a brand new hop on the market, having just been released in 1993. (It had some limited distribution before then as CFJ-Hallertau.) It is one of three "sister hops" that were bred from Hallertauer Mittelfrüh (the other two are Mt. Hood and Liberty). It is the third and latest hop to be released in the US breeding program to duplicate the characteristics of Hallertauer Mittelfrüh in a hop that would grow well in the US. In ranking the three hops for closeness to Hallertauer Mittelfrüh, Crystal is tied with Liberty, with Mt. Hood coming in a very close second. Being new on the market, it is too early to tell how popular Crystal will be, but so far brewers have been quite pleased with it. For the next few years, Crystal will be somewhat hard to find, but availability will improve as the planted acreage grows and as popularity and awareness increases.

Alpha Acids (typical): 2-4.5%

Beta Acids (typical): 4.5-6.5%

Alpha/Beta Ratio: 0.6

Cohumulone % (typical): 20-26%

Total Oil % (typical): 1.0-1.5%

Myrcene % (typical): 40-50%

Humulene % (typical): 20-30%

Humulene/Caryophyllene Ratio: 3.5

Aroma: Mild and pleasant with a "noble" character.

Storage: Poor. 49% alpha acids lost after 6 months at 20°C.

Country of Origin: USA, grown primarily in Oregon.

Usage: Crystal is appropriate for all lagers, especially those known for their use of "noble" hops. These include both American (megabrewery and microbrewery) and German lagers. Some brewers believe that Liberty is too spicy, and Mt. Hood not noble enough, and these brewers have been pleased with Crystal.

Substitutes: Liberty, Mt. Hood and Hallertauer Mittelfrüh, if you could get it! Hallertau Hersbrucker is also a possibility. Please note that domestic Hallertau is *not* a close substitute.

Czech Saaz: Czech Saaz (or Saazer) is the only real noble hop that is somewhat available to homebrewers. Grown in what used to be Czechoslovakia (and is now the Czech Republic), it is the signature hop of all authentic Pilsners, with Pilsner Urquell being the most famous. Pronounced sahz or sahts.

Alpha Acids (typical): 3-4.5%

Beta Acids (typical): 3-4%

Alpha/Beta Ratio: 1

Cohumulone % (typical): 24-28%

Total Oil % (typical): 0.4-0.7%

Myrcene % (typical): 20-25%

Humulene % (typical): 40-45%

Humulene/Caryophyllene Ratio: 3.8

Aroma: Very mild and noble, with pleasant hoppy notes.

Storage: Poor. 50% alpha acids lost after 6 months at 20°C.

Country of Origin: Czech Republic (formerly Czechoslovakia).

Usage: If you want to make an authentic Bohemian Pilsner, you need to use Czech Saaz in the finish and preferably as the only hop.

Substitutes: If you can't find Czech Saaz, then Polish Lublin or Lubelski can be used, but this will most likely be harder to find. Spalt Spalter or the newer Spalter Select are very Saaz-like. In a pinch, try some Tettnanger, or even Liberty. Domestic Saaz is considered by some brewers to be an acceptable substitute, but other brewers say just the opposite. But really, there is nothing like Czech Saaz for an authentic Pilsner.

East Kent Goldings: Goldings is actually a whole family
of hops that have evolved from a seedling selected by Mr.
Golding in the 1800s. They are grown in the area of Kent,
England, with those from the East part of Kent being the most
highly prized. East Kent Goldings is the premier English aroma
hop, and should always be your first choice for any English-style
beer from Stouts to Milds. Be prepared to put up with a
significantly higher quantity of stems than you would expect in
domestic hops. Some seeds may also be present.

Alpha Acids (typical): 4.0-5.5%

Beta Acids (typical): 2.0-3.5%

Alpha/Beta Ratio: 2.3

Cohumulone % (typical): 20-25%

Total Oil % (typical): 0.3-1%

Myrcene % (typical): 20-26%

Humulene % (typical): 42-48%

Humulene/Caryophyllene Ratio: 3.5

Aroma: Mild, pleasant and slightly flowery.

Storage: Poor. 45% alpha acids lost after 6 months at 20°C.

Country of Origin: England.

Usage: Can you say English Ales? I'm sure you can! Needless
to say, this is *the* hop to use for all English-style Ales, including
Milds, Bitters (Pale Ales), India Pale Ales, Porters and even
Stouts. If you want to make sure the character of this hop comes
through, use it as the sole hop, for bittering as well as finishing,
or use a lot in the finish. For Pale Ales or IPAs, dry hop with
East Kent Goldings for extra aroma (and authenticity).

Substitutes: English Fuggle is the first choice. B.C. Goldings
would be second. Then, in order of preference, domestic Fuggle
or Willamette. Please note that Styrian Goldings is not a
Goldings variety, but is actually Fuggle. Also note that Brewer's
Gold is an entirely different hop, and not a substitute at all.

Fuggle: Fuggle is a classic English aroma hop, second in popularity to East Kent Goldings. If you can get it, real English Fuggle is superior to domestic Fuggle, but the latter is still quite good. Be prepared to find seeds in English Fuggle, and occasionally in domestic Fuggle as well. Pronounced fuh´-gull (not foo´-gull).

Alpha Acids (typical): English: 4.5-5.5% Domestic: 4-5.5%

Beta Acids (typical): English: 2.5-3% Domestic: 1.5-2%

Alpha/Beta Ratio: English: 1.8 Domestic: 2.7

Cohumulone % (typical): English: 26% Domestic: 25-32%

Total Oil % (typical): English: 1.4% Domestic: 0.7-1.2%

Myrcene % (typical): English: 24-28% Domestic: 40-50%

Humulene % (typical): English: 35-40% Domestic: 20-26%

Humulene/Caryophyllene Ratio: English: 3.3 Domestic: 2.9

Aroma: Mild and pleasant, with the English having the edge over the domestic.

Storage: Fair. 35% alpha acids lost after 6 months at 20°C.

Country of Origin: England, but also widely grown in the US.

Usage: Fuggle is appropriate in all English-style Ales, including Milds, Bitters (Pale Ales), India Pale Ales, Porters and even Stouts. If you want to make sure the character of this hop comes through, use it as the sole hop, for bittering as well as finishing, or use a lot in the finish.

Substitutes: If you can't get English Fuggle, domestic Fuggle is a good substitute. Styrian Goldings are actually Fuggle grown in Slovenia, and they would be a fine substitute but more expensive. Willamette is a seedless version of Fuggle, and it is just slightly spicier in character. Lastly, East Kent or B.C. Goldings are considered superior to Fuggle and would certainly be appropriate in any style where Fuggle was used.

Hallertauer (domestic): Domestic Hallertauer is
Hallertauer Mittelfrüh grown here. Rootstocks were simply
imported from Germany and planted in the Pacific Northwest.
The problem with this strategy is that it just doesn't grow the
same in the US, and consequently the brewing characteristics
aren't quite the same as real Hallertauer Mittelfrüh. Nevertheless,
many brewers like this hop (whether or not it's simply because
they think they're getting a noble hop is another issue).
Pronounced like the words "holler" (like you holler at someone)
and "tower" (like an ivory tower) with the accent on the first
syllable.

Alpha Acids (typical): 3.5-4.5%

Beta Acids (typical): 3.5-4.5%

Alpha/Beta Ratio: 1

Cohumulone % (typical): 18-24%

Total Oil % (typical): 0.6-1%

Myrcene % (typical): 35-44%

Humulene % (typical): 41-48%

Humulene/Caryophyllene Ratio: 3

Aroma: Mild, pleasant and slightly flowery.

Storage: Poor. 45% alpha acids lost after 6 months at 20°C.

Country of Origin: Germany, but grown in limited quantities
here.

Usage: German lagers and ales.

Substitutes: If you are using *this* hop as a substitute for
Hallertauer Mittelfrüh, then you would be better off with
Crystal, Liberty or Mt. Hood. Another good choice would be
Hallertau Hersbrucker or the newer Hallertauer Tradition.

Hallertau Hersbrucker: This variety originated in the
Hersbruck region of Germany, but is now widely grown in the
Hallertau. It had replaced a good deal of the Hallertauer
Mittelfrüh acreage because it has a good aroma profile and is
not susceptible to the verticillium wilt that inhabits the region.
German hop brokers and growers keep trying to elevate this hop
to noble status, but they aren't having much success. Still,
Hallertau Hersbrucker has a fine aroma and is widely used in
German beers. Growers in the Hallertau are reportedly replacing
nearly all the Hersbrucker acreage with Hallertauer Tradition and
Spalter Select, so this hop is becoming harder to get. For a
pronunciation of Hallertau, see Hallertauer above, and leave off
the "er" on the end. Hersbrucker is pronounced like it looks:
hehrs´-bruh-kehr or to be really German, hairs´-bruh-kehr.

Alpha Acids (typical): 3-5.5%

Beta Acids (typical): 4-5.5%

Alpha/Beta Ratio: 1

Cohumulone % (typical): 19-25%

Total Oil % (typical): 0.7-1.3%

Myrcene % (typical): 15-25%

Humulene % (typical): 15-25%

Humulene/Caryophyllene Ratio: 2.1

Aroma: Mild to semi-strong, while capturing a good deal of "nobleness".

Storage: Fair. 40% alpha acids lost after 6 months at 20°C.

Country of Origin: Germany

Usage: Appropriate in all German lagers and ales.

Substitutes: Crystal, Liberty or Mt. Hood, unless you can get Hallertauer Mittelfrüh (good luck!).

Hallertauer Mittelfrüh: From the viewpoint of US breweries,

Hallertauer Mittelfrüh was the most important noble hop. It is more correctly called Hallertau Hallertauer Mittelfrüh, but that's a mouthful, so the first Hallertau is usually dropped. Demand for this hop is so high that the entire Hallertau could be devoted to this single variety and still not enough could be grown. But only about 20% of the Hallertau acreage produces this hop and that is diminishing yearly. Why? Because it is highly susceptible to the strain of verticillium wilt that inhabits the Hallertau. The acreage left is mostly controlled by the US and European megabreweries. This means that there is never any Hallertauer Mittelfrüh available to microbrewers or homebrewers. Luckily for us, there are some decent substitutes. For a pronunciation of Hallertauer, see the entry under Hallertauer. Mittelfrüh is pronounced mih´-tehl-frue.

Alpha Acids (typical): 3.5-5.5%

Beta Acids (typical): 3.5-5.5%

Alpha/Beta Ratio: 1

Cohumulone % (typical): 21%

Total Oil % (typical): 1%

Myrcene % (typical): 32%

Humulene % (typical): 40%

Humulene/Caryophyllene Ratio: 3.7

Aroma: Very fine, noble aroma.

Storage: Poor. 45% of alpha acids lost after 6 months at 20°C.

Country of Origin: Germany.

Usage: All lagers (perhaps with the exception of pilsners), especially German lagers. The Boston Beer Company's Samuel Adams Lager claims to have a high percentage of Hallertauer Mittelfrüh in the hop bill and is even dry hopped with it.

Substitutes: If you want to stay with a German hop, try the new Hallertauer Tradition if you can find it. Crystal, Liberty and Mt. Hood are all good domestic substitutes. Note that domestic Hallertau is *not* a very good substitute.

Hallertauer Tradition: This is a new aroma hop on the market that was bred in Germany as a disease resistant and higher yielding version of Hallertauer Mittelfrüh. It is grown in mainly in the Hallertau and therefore would be called Hallertau Hallertauer Tradition. The rumor is that the major US consumers of Hallertauer Mittelfrüh have instructed the hop growers in the Hallertau that they can ship Hallertauer Tradition as a replacement. And the growers have reportedly responded by replacing most Hallertauer Mittelfrüh and Hersbrucker acreage with Hallertauer Tradition. So we are likely to see a lot of this hop in the US market. For a pronunciation of Hallertauer, see the entry under Hallertauer.

Alpha Acids (typical): 5-7%%

Beta Acids (typical): 4-5%

Alpha/Beta Ratio: 1.3

Cohumulone % (typical): 26-29%

Total Oil % (typical): 1-1.4%

Myrcene % (typical): 20-25%

Humulene % (typical): 45-55%

Humulene/Caryophyllene Ratio: 4.1

Aroma: Very fine, noble aroma.

Storage: No exact data yet, but reported to be good.

Country of Origin: Germany.

Usage: All lagers (perhaps with the exception of pilsners), especially German lagers.

Substitutes: Crystal, Liberty and Mt. Hood are all good domestic substitutes. Note that domestic Hallertau is *not* a very good substitute.

Hersbrucker (domestic): Domestic Hersbrucker is the
German Hersbrucker variety grown in the US. It has a lighter
aroma than Hallertau Hersbrucker, and is even less "noble". Not
very widely planted, but it does show up in homebrew supply
stores often. Just make sure you don't think that a hop simply
labeled "Hersbrucker" is imported.

Alpha Acids (typical): 3.5-5.5%

Beta Acids (typical): 5.5-7%

Alpha/Beta Ratio: 0.7

Cohumulone % (typical): 20-30%

Total Oil % (typical): 0.6-1.2%

Myrcene % (typical): 40-50%

Humulene % (typical): 20-30%

Humulene/Caryophyllene Ratio: 1.8

Aroma: Light, clean and somewhat spicy. Less noble than
Hallertau Hersbrucker, which itself is less noble than
Hallertauer Mittelfrüh, so domestic Hersbrucker is getting
pretty far away.

Storage: Fair. 40% alpha acids lost after 6 months at 20°C.

Country of Origin: Germany, but grown here in limited
quantities.

Usage: German lagers and ales.

Substitutes: Hallertau Hersbrucker is superior. Crystal,
Liberty or Mt. Hood would most likely be in style for any recipe
calling for Hersbrucker, but they will have different aroma
characteristics.

Hüller Bitterer: Even though it's name implies different,

Hüller Bitterer is an aroma hop, bred in Germany (by the hop researchers at Hüll) as a replacement for Hallertauer Mittelfrüh that was more disease resistant (it succeeded on that count, but didn't measure up in the aroma department). It was widely planted for a while, but has now largely been replaced with Perle and Hersbrucker. Hüller Bitterer is sometimes referred to simply as Hüller, probably because it really is an aroma hop. I would normally not have included it, but I have seen it show up recently at a few homebrew shops. Pronounced: hue´-ler.

Alpha Acids (typical): 4.5-7%

Beta Acids (typical): 4-6%

Alpha/Beta Ratio: 1.2

Cohumulone % (typical): 30%

Total Oil % (typical): 1.2%

Myrcene % (typical): 51%

Humulene % (typical): 9%

Humulene/Caryophyllene Ratio: 1.9

Aroma: Moderate, not objectionable, but not much information available.

Storage: Fair. 40% of alpha acids lost after 6 months at 20°C.

Country of Origin: Germany

Usage: German lagers and ales. Can be used for bittering or aroma, but better hops are available for both.

Substitutes: Perle, Hallertau Hersbrucker.

Liberty:
Liberty is a relatively new hop on the market, but is already gaining much success with brewers. It is one of three "sister hops" that were bred from Hallertauer Mittelfrüh (the other two are Mt. Hood and Crystal). It was the second hop to be released in the US breeding program to duplicate the characteristics of Hallertauer Mittelfrüh in a hop that would grow well in the US. In ranking the three hops for closeness to Hallertauer Mittelfrüh, Liberty is tied with Crystal, with Mt. Hood coming in a very close second.

Alpha Acids (typical): 3-5%

Beta Acids (typical): 3-4%

Alpha/Beta Ratio: 1.1

Cohumulone % (typical): 24-30%

Total Oil % (typical): 0.6-1.2%

Myrcene % (typical): 35-40%

Humulene % (typical): 35-40%

Humulene/Caryophyllene Ratio: 3.7

Aroma: Mild and pleasant with definite noble characteristics, especially after some aging. Some spicy notes.

Storage: Poor. 55% alpha acids lost after 6 months at 20°C.

Country of Origin: USA, grown primarily in Oregon.

Usage: Liberty is appropriate for all lagers, especially those known for their use of "noble" hops. These include both American (megabrewery and microbrewery) and German lagers. Pete's Wicked Lager features Liberty. If the slight extra spiciness bothers you, use one of the recommended substitutes.

Substitutes: Crystal or Mt. Hood, with Crystal being slightly closer. Since Liberty was designed as a substitute for Hallertauer Mittelfrüh, you could use it, if you could get it! Hallertau Hersbrucker or Hallertauer Tradition are also possibilities. Please note that domestic Hallertau is *not* a very good substitute.

Lubelski or Lublin: It is unclear whether these are two
separate varieties or just one with different names. In any case,
they are so close that we can consider them together as if they
were one variety. Lubelski (Lublin) is the same variety as Czech
Saaz, but grown in Poland. Although it really deserves noble
status, it isn't technically a noble hop. Now and then, Lublin
appears on the micro and homebrewing scene, and if there's no
Czech Saaz available, this is a good choice. Pronounced lew-
behl´-skee or lewb´-lihn.

Alpha Acids (typical): 3-5%

Beta Acids (typical): 2.3-3.8%

Alpha/Beta Ratio: 1.3

Cohumulone % (typical): 27%

Total Oil % (typical): 1%

Myrcene % (typical): 25-35%

Humulene % (typical): 35-40%

Humulene/Caryophyllene Ratio: 3.7

Aroma: Very mild and noble, with pleasant hoppy notes.

Storage: Fair. 40% alpha acids lost after 6 months at 20°C.

Country of Origin: Originally from Czechoslovakia, but this
variety grown in Poland.

Usage: Use any place you would use Czech Saaz.

Substitutes: Czech Saaz, Spalter Select, or in a pinch Tettnanger.

Mt. Hood: Mt. Hood was the first hop to be released in the
US breeding program to duplicate the characteristics of
Hallertauer Mittelfrüh in a hop that would grow well in the US.
It was the first of three "sister" hops, the other two being Crystal
and Liberty. In ranking the three hops for closeness to Hallertauer
Mittelfrüh, Liberty is tied with Crystal, with Mt. Hood coming
in a very close second. The trial plots of Mt. Hood were very
encouraging as to the closeness to Hallertauer Mittelfrüh, but the
commercial plots have not lived up to expectations. This was
thought to be due to drastically different weather conditions in
the years following the trial growths. In 1993, the weather
conditions in the Pacific Northwest were back to normal, and
the 1993 Mt. Hood crop was far more noble in character than
previous years. So we now may be back to a toss-up on all three
sisters.

Alpha Acids (typical): 5-8%

Beta Acids (typical): 5-7.5%

Alpha/Beta Ratio: 1

Cohumulone % (typical): 22-23%

Total Oil % (typical): 1-1.3%

Myrcene % (typical): 55-65%

Humulene % (typical): 15-25%

Humulene/Caryophyllene Ratio: 2.3

Aroma: Mild, pleasant and clean, definite noble character.

Storage: Poor. 45% alpha acids lost after 6 months at 20°C.

Country of Origin: USA, grown primarily in Oregon.

Usage: Mt. Hood is appropriate for all lagers, especially those
known for their use of "noble" hops. These include both
American (megabrewery and microbrewery) and German
lagers.

Substitutes: Crystal or Liberty. Since Mt. Hood was designed
as a substitute for Hallertauer Mittelfrüh, you could use it, if
you could get it! You might try the new Hallertauer Tradition.
Please note that domestic Hallertau is *not* a very good
substitute.

Saazer (domestic):

Saazer (domestic): Domestic Saazer is Czech Saaz grown in the US. Unfortunately, like Hallertauer Mittelfrüh, it doesn't do as well here as it does in its native land. Despite the fact that domestic Saazer bears only some resemblance to real Czech Saaz, it seems to command a premium price due to its low yield. In my opinion, you would do better to try and find real Czech Saaz. Having said all that, a lot of brewers like this hop. Pronounced sahtz´-ehr.

Alpha Acids (typical): 4.3%

Beta Acids (typical): 3.6%

Alpha/Beta Ratio: 1.2

Cohumulone % (typical): 24%

Total Oil % (typical): 0.6%

Myrcene % (typical): 37%

Humulene % (typical): 23%

Humulene/Caryophyllene Ratio: 3.4

Aroma: Good, but nothing like Czech Saaz.

Storage: Poor. 50% alpha acids lost after 6 months at 20°C.

Country of Origin: Czechoslovakia, but also grown in the US on a very limited basis.

Usage: Pilsners.

Substitutes: Real Czech Saaz is superior. Polish Lublin, Spalt Spalter and Spalter Select would also be good substitutes..

67

Spalt Spalter:

Spalt Spalter (usually shortened to just Spalt, Spalter or called German Spalter) is one of the "noble" hops. Spalter is a land race variety named after the area in which it is grown (Spalt) and it is not really grown anywhere else in Germany. Production is small, but it is available to home and micro brewers from time to time. Pronounced shpawl´-tehr (the German way) or spawl´-tehr (the English way).

Alpha Acids (typical): 4-5.5%

Beta Acids (typical): 4-5.5%

Alpha/Beta Ratio: 1

Cohumulone % (typical): 22-28%

Total Oil % (typical): 0.5-1.1%

Myrcene % (typical): 15 25%

Humulene % (typical): 18-20%

Humulene/Caryophyllene Ratio: 1.7

Aroma: Mild, pleasant and very noble in character. Slightly spicy.

Storage: Poor. 55% of alpha acids lost after 6 months at 20°C.

Country of Origin: Germany.

Usage: German lagers or other beers where noble hops are appropriate.

Substitutes: If you want to stay with a German hop, the new variety Spalter Select is probably your best bet. Domestic Spalter, Czech Saaz or Tettnanger are also possibilities. Crystal, Liberty and Mt. Hood won't be the same, but probably won't be out of style.

Spalter (domestic):
The fine German aroma hop, grown in the US. Again, like most of the other German and European varieties, the brewing characteristics of the domestic grown Spalter are not as good as the real thing. Domestic Spalter is not very widely grown, and hardly ever shows up in the homebrewing trade. It is also not a very high yielding crop, so growers prefer to plant something that yields better. Pronounced shpawl´-tehr (the German way) or spawl´-tehr (the English way).

Alpha Acids (typical): 3-6%

Beta Acids (typical): 3-5%

Alpha/Beta Ratio: 1.1

Cohumulone % (typical): 20-25%

Total Oil % (typical): 0.5-1%

Myrcene % (typical): 35-55%

Humulene % (typical): 10-20%

Humulene/Caryophyllene Ratio: 3

Aroma: Mild and pleasant, but doesn't compare to German Spalter.

Storage: Poor. 50% of alpha acids lost after 6 months at 20°C.

Country of Origin: Germany, but grown to limited extent in the US.

Usage: German lagers or other beers where noble hops are appropriate.

Substitutes: German Spalter, Spalter Select or Czech Saaz are superior. For domestic substitutes, try Tettnanger or possibly Liberty.

Spalter Select: This is a relatively new hop variety on the market.

It was bred as a disease resistant and higher yielding version of the Spalter hop. It is grown primarily in the Hallertau, so then it would be called Hallertau Spalter Select. It is reportedly very similar to Czech Saaz in aroma. The word from Germany is that this hop is now widely planted in the Hallertau, so we should be seeing quite a bit of it in the years to come. Pronounced shpawl´-tehr (the German way) or spawl´-tehr (the English way).

Alpha Acids (typical): 4-6%

Beta Acids (typical): 3.5-4.5%

Alpha/Beta Ratio: 1.2

Cohumulone % (typical): 21-25%

Total Oil % (typical): 0.5-1%

Myrcene % (typical): 15-25%

Humulene % (typical): 15-25%

Humulene/Caryophyllene Ratio: ? ?

Aroma: Very fine, reportedly close to Czech Saaz (as is Spalter).

Storage: No exact data yet, but reported to be good.

Country of Origin: Germany, but grown to limited extent in the US.

Usage: German lagers or other beers where noble hops are appropriate.

Substitutes: German Spalter, Tettnanger, or Czech Saaz.

Styrian Goldings: Styrian (or Savinja) Goldings are actually Fuggle, grown in Slovenia. While it is a fine hop, it is *not* Goldings. It compares approximately with domestic Fuggle, which is going to be much more economical and easier to come by. No one is quite sure who is to blame for calling it Goldings (some say it is the Slovenian hop merchants, some blame the English hop exporters who, allegedly, sold the Slovenians "Fuggles Goldings"). In any case, the motive was clear: Goldings was more highly prized than Fuggle, thus Styrian Goldings commands a higher price than would "Styrian Fuggle". To this day, the scheme still works (but now you know!). Another interesting fact about this hop's name is that one would assume "Styria" is the place where the hops were grown. But Styria is in Austria, not Slovenia. I guess Styrian Goldings has a much better ring to it than "Slovenian Fuggles".

Alpha Acids (typical): 4.5-6%

Beta Acids (typical): 2.3-3%

Alpha/Beta Ratio: 2

Cohumulone % (typical): 28%

Total Oil % (typical): 0.8%

Myrcene % (typical): 27-33%

Humulene % (typical): 34-38%

Humulene/Caryophyllene Ratio: 3.1

Aroma: Mild and pleasant, very similar to domestic Fuggle.

Storage: Good. 37% of alpha acids lost after 6 months at 20°C.

Country of Origin: Originally from England, but this variety grown in Slovenia.

Usage: Same as Fuggle, which means all English-style beers.

Substitutes: English Fuggle would be superior, as would any real Goldings variety. Domestic Fuggle or Willamette would be good alternatives, and more economical.

Tettnang Tettnanger:
Tettnang Tettnanger is one of the four genuine noble hops. It is a land race variety, named after the Tettnang region around Lake Constance in Germany. Tettnang Tettnanger is rarely available to home and microbrewers, but occasionally it does make an appearance. Pronounced: teht´-nang-ehr (rhymes with "wet hanger", and has a hard "g").

Alpha Acids (typical): 3.5-5.5%

Beta Acids (typical): 3.5-5%

Alpha/Beta Ratio: 1

Cohumulone % (typical): 23-29%

Total Oil % (typical): 0.6-1%

Myrcene % (typical): 20-25%

Humulene % (typical): 20-25%

Humulene/Caryophyllene Ratio: 3

Aroma: Mild, pleasant and noble. Slightly spicy.

Storage: Poor. 42% alpha acids lost after 6 months at 20°C.

Country of Origin: Germany.

Usage: German lagers and ales, and would also be appropriate in domestic "premium lagers", but usually it would be used in conjunction with other noble-type hops. The Boston Beer Company's Samuel Adams Lager reportedly has some Tettnang Tettnanger in the hop bill, but the percentage is unknown (the bulk is reportedly Hallertauer Mittelfrüh).

Substitutes: Unlike the other noble hops, domestic Tettnanger is not a bad substitute for the Tettnang Tettnanger. Other possibilities would be Spalt Spalter, Spalter Select or Czech Saaz.

Tettnanger (domestic): The noble hop Tettnang Tettnanger, but grown in the US. Unlike most other European varieties, Tettnanger does reasonably well here. I don't hesitate to recommend it if you can't get Tettnang Tettnanger, which is almost always the case. Pronounced: teht´-nang-ehr (rhymes with "wet hanger", and has a hard "g").

Alpha Acids (typical): 4-5%

Beta Acids (typical): 3-4%

Alpha/Beta Ratio: 1.3

Cohumulone % (typical): 20-25%

Total Oil % (typical): 0.4-0.8%

Myrcene % (typical): 36-45%

Humulene % (typical): 18-23%

Humulene/Caryophyllene Ratio: 3.1

Aroma: Mild, pleasant and noble. Slightly spicy.

Storage: Poor. 42% of alpha acids lost after 6 months at 20°C.

Country of Origin: Germany, but now grown in the US quite successfully.

Usage: German lagers and ales, and would also be appropriate in domestic "premium lagers", but usually it would be used in conjunction with other noble-type hops.

Substitutes: German Spalt, Spalter Select or Czech Saaz, or if you can get it, why not use Tettnang Tettnanger?

73

Willamette: Willamette is a seedless triploid version of Fuggle, and has nearly identical brewing characteristics to domestic Fuggle. Willamette has become quite a popular hop with homebrewers and microbrewers alike, and is well established in the industry.

Alpha Acids (typical): 4-6%

Beta Acids (typical): 3-4%

Alpha/Beta Ratio: 1.4

Cohumulone % (typical): 30-35%

Total Oil % (typical): 1-1.5%

Myrcene % (typical): 45-55%

Humulene % (typical): 20-30%

Humulene/Caryophyllene Ratio: 3.3

Aroma: Mild and pleasant, with a slight spicy note missing in Fuggle.

Storage: Fair. 37% of alpha acids lost after 6 months at 20°C.

Country of Origin: USA, grown primarily in Oregon.

Usage: Willamette is appropriate for all English-style ales, including Milds and Bitters (Pale Ales), India Pale Ales, Porters and Stouts. It is also used in quite a few American-style Ales. Personally, I think Willamette gives beers a slight metallic taste that I don't get with Fuggle, especially when Willamette is used to dry hop a beer. But I am the only one I know that tastes this (so far). But if your beer has a metallic taste, and you've eliminated all the normal causes for this, it could be the Willamette.

Substitutes: Fuggle, domestic or imported, or Styrian Goldings. For a superior substitute, try East Kent Goldings.

Chapter 5 - Hop Products and Processing

In this chapter we will talk about what happens to the hops from the time of harvest and how they are processed into a form that is ready for use in brewing. The amount of processing depends on the form that the products take: Whole hops, pellets, plugs or extracts of some sort. We will describe these products and discuss the relative merits and uses of them.

Hop Harvesting and Drying

All hops are harvested once per year, beginning in mid-August and continuing through early September (in the northern hemisphere), depending on the hop variety. Most hops are machine picked these days, but some hop farms in Europe still use hand picking. In any case, the bine is usually cut down and either picked by hand or fed into a "hop picker" which strips the cones from bines and separates out most of the leaf and stem material.

Once the cones have been separated from the bine, the hops are dried in buildings known in England as *oast houses* or in the US as *hop kilns*. The actual equipment and

Mechanical hop harvesting. The vines are taken down, placed in a cart and hauled indoors where the cones are removed.
Photo courtesy of Dave Wills.

facilities can vary widely, but essentially the process consists of spreading the cones out on a screen and passing hot air through them. The hops are dried until only about 8% of the moisture remains. Hops start out with about 80% moisture, so if you had 1 pound of freshly picked hops (called *green hops*) after drying they would weigh only about 3.5 ozs.

It used to be common practice in the USA and Europe to "sulfur" the hops during drying. This was done by burning sulfur and mixing the sulfur fumes with the hot air used to dry the hops. The sulfur has the effect of "greening up" the hops to give them a better appearance. The practice has now been discontinued and is actually prohibited in most countries.

Once the hops are dried, in the US they are baled into 200 lb bales. The bales are made by compressing the hops to about 3-4 times their original volume and then wrapped in burlap to keep the bale compressed. It Europe, the hops

Inside a modern hop kiln where the hops are dried.
Photo by Ulrich Gampert.

will typically be pressed into balloon-shaped "pockets" that weigh about 110 lbs. These are large burlap bags that are stuffed with hops through about three filling and compression cycles. In Europe, hop quantities are commonly expressed in *zentners*, which equal 50 kg or 110 lbs, and are sometimes sold this way.

Typically, all of the processing described so far (picking, drying and baling) will be done by the hop farmer/grower. At this point, the hops will be sold directly to a brewery that has contracted directly with the grower (usually done only by major breweries), or, as is most often the case, sold to a hop broker. Probably a good 80-90% of the world's hop supplies pass through a broker.

The Hop Broker

The hop broker plays a very important role in handling and processing the hops. The first job of the hop broker is to physically inspect the hops for any problems.

The hop broker's first examination of the hops begins with a visual inspection. Photo by Ulrich Gampert.

Hops are either accepted or rejected based on the quality of the hop. The hops are then analyzed for alpha acids, oil content, aroma, appearance and host of other factors, then sorted into lots based on these criteria. Each lot is assigned a number and the data for that lot is recorded.

As the lots are being made up, some of the major breweries visit the hop broker to pick the lots they want to buy. One may think that if the major breweries get to pick their lots first, us home and microbrewers get left with the dregs. That is not the case (at least in the US, I can't say for Europe). In fact, the hop brokers will typically reserve some of the best lots of hops for the microbrewers, and it is from these same lots that hop suppliers catering to the homebrew trade also buy.

Up until this point, the hops have remained in their full bales. If a brewer uses whole hops (also known as raw hops or by the misnomer leaf hops), they will be bought in this form. But the majority of micro brewers use the hops in pellet form. The hop broker will take a portion of the whole hops and have them processed into pellets. In England, some of the hops will be pressed into plugs. And in Germany, the hops may be super-compressed into 11 lb (5 kg) bricks. Some of the hops will also be processed into extracts. All of these products will be discussed in detail, but the point here is that typically it is the hop broker that makes all of these decisions, and performs (or contracts for) all of this processing.

The hops sold to the major breweries are generally shipped off to the breweries where they take care of storing the hops until they are used. The remaining hops are then stored in huge warehouses just below freezing (this temperature differs depending on the broker, and the outside temperature). They stay there until they are shipped to either a brewer or hop supplier. Most small brewers buy enough hops at the start of the hop season to last all year, but they are stored in the hop broker's warehouses and shipped periodically to the brewer. This keeps the brewer from needing a huge cold storage facility. Also, since most small brewers don't have hop analysis equipment, this allows the hop broker to keep tabs on the alpha acid and oil contents as they change over time.

To summarize, the hop broker provides many important services. They inspect the hops, store them, analyze them for alpha acid content and process them into the various hop products.

Crop Years

Hops are harvested once a year, and they start showing up in homebrew shops in the last few months of the year in which they were harvested. For example, hops harvested in 1993 (called the '93 Crop) will show up near the end of 1993. They will be sold until the end of 1994. So the crop year always seems a year out of date. The only exception to this are hops from Australia and New Zealand, which are harvested in March.

Hops from Europe can take considerably longer to show up here. They will start to arrive in late December and continue to trickle in until April or later.

Whole Hops

When hops are used directly from the bale, they are called either whole hops or raw hops. (I prefer the term whole hops, so that is what I'll use from now on.) They are often called leaf hops (or even worse, whole leaf hops), but the leaves of the hop plant are not what we use in brewing. We use the flowers, and sometimes you see the complete term "whole hop flowers" used, though by the time we get them a good portion of the flowers aren't whole anymore.

Whole hops are the least processed form of hops, and are the traditional way that hops were used. Some brewers believe that whole hops provide the best aroma, and the lack of processing may provide some basis for that belief. Although the flowers have been smashed flat by the baling process, most of the lupulin glands are still intact.

When the homebrewer buys whole hops, there is usually very little evidence left of the baling process, except for the fact that the hop cones are flattened. Sometimes a few chunks of hops are still pressed together, but in general the hops have re-expanded to near their original volume. This is a consequence of handling by the hop supplier, who will have separated the hops from the bale to weigh and bag them.

The biggest disadvantage of whole hops is the amount

Hops are compressed into 200 lb bales and wrapped in burlap.
Photo by Ulrich Gampert.

of space they consume. In the days before oxygen barrier packaging and refrigerated storage, whole hops used to be in pretty sorry shape by the time you bought them. Pellets have a reputation for being fresher, and in the past there was good reason to believe it. But now it is quite possible for the homebrewer to buy really fresh whole hops, so there is no reason to reject them on "freshness" reasons. I believe their biggest advantage is that they are much easier to filter out of the wort, and I also enjoy the "aesthetics" of whole hops. But you need to judge for yourself, and more importantly, match the form of hops to your brewing equipment and technique (more on this later).

Hop Pellets

Hop pellets look just like rabbit food pellets, in fact they are made with the same type of process and machine. To make hop pellets, the hops are first ground into a powder. This must be done very carefully so that heat doesn't build up and cause too much of the hop resins to be lost or destroyed. The result is a fine powder of hop particles. The hop powder is then pressed and extruded though a pellet die, again taking care not to heat the hops too much while doing this. The hop resins act as a built-in binder to cause the particles to stick together. If the bond was really strong, what would come out of the pellet die would resemble "hop spaghetti" but the weight of the extruded hops causes them to naturally break into pellets.

The hop pellets are then packaged into large (usually 44 lb) foil bags and vacuum sealed. The resulting bag takes up less than 1/4 the space of the whole hops. Because they are now vacuum sealed, the hops will have a better storage life. Because they take up so little space compared to whole hops, a homebrew dealer can stock a wider variety of pellets than whole hops and not have to buy lots of freezers or coolers to display and store them in. Microbrewers can now stock a fair supply of different varieties while taking up only a few square feet in the keg cooler.

But something has to be lost in the pelletizing process. In fact, about 4-6% of the alpha acids and oils are lost. Some brewers believe that in this 4-6%, some intangible "goodness" has been lost, and therefore prefer whole hops to pellets. You'll have to judge for yourself. In any case, you don't have to account for these losses: the alpha acid rating (and if available, the oil content rating) is done after the pelletizing process.

There are actually several types of hop pellets on the market. The most common is the Type 90 pellet. As

Above is the hammer mill that grinds the whole hops into a powder. At the left is a pellet press where the powder is made into hop pellets. Photos courtesy of Hopunion USA, Inc.

described above, the Type 90 pellets are simply the whole hops, ground and pelletized. Sometimes on the market are the Type 45 pellets, which are also called *enriched pellets* because part of the "inert" hop material is removed prior to pelletizing. This is an entirely mechanical process and not done with any chemical extraction. Typically, Type 45 pellets have about twice as much alpha acid as the same weight of Type 90 pellets. There are also "stabilized" and "pre-isomerized" pellets on the market, but these are rarely encountered. The alpha acids in these pellets have been treated chemically. In the stabilized pellets, magnesium has been added to partially isomerize the alpha acids, and in the pre-isomerized pellets, virtually all of the alphas have been converted to iso-alpha acids. Both are attempts to get better utilization and/or decrease the time needed for boiling. You'll probably never encounter these last two, but if you do, I would advise against using them for late additions or dry hopping, as normally these processes don't add significant amounts of iso-alpha acids to the beer. But the stabilized or pre-isomerized pellets will, so that will make your beer unaccountably bitter.

When pellets are introduced to the brew kettle, they immediately disintegrate back into powder. The process of pelletizing bursts most of the lupulin glands, so pellets will give a better extraction rate than whole hops for short boil or contact times. For longer times (greater than 30 minutes) the difference is negligible.

Hop Plugs and Bricks

The hop plug has recently become popular on the homebrewing scene, but has actually been in use in the UK as a convenient means of dry hopping cask conditioned ales. The hop plug is technically a Type 100 pellet, and is made by compressing whole hops (unground) into a plug that measures about 1" across and about 1/2" thick and weighs approximately 1/2 oz.

The hop plug is compressed to the point where, as with the other pellets, the resins hold the plug together. The hops take up only about 1/3 the space of whole hops, and are easier to store and package. When the plug is introduced into the brew kettle, the hops re-expand and behave and look just like whole hops. It can sometimes take quite a few minutes to break apart, so this can be a factor if your contact time is short, like at the end of the boil.

The plugs are a reasonable compromise between whole hops and pellets, but they are not without their own problems. If you always add hops in 1/2 oz increments, the plugs are great. But if you need a portion of a plug, they are very difficult to break apart. The weight of the plug varies a bit too, they are only *approximately* half an ounce. It would also seem that it is easy to keep the plugs fresh, but as of this writing, the only plug-making machines were in England. For English varieties, this should be great: harvest, plug and package. But for domestic varieties, the hops need to be shipped to England, plugged and then shipped back again, and this has the possibility of negating any freshness advantages. Lastly, the plugs cost a lot more than either whole hops or pellets. As of this writing, there was only one company actively marketing plugs in the US, but that is likely to change. Hopefully, the quality and pricing will improve when more suppliers get involved.

I have mentioned the 11 lb bricks of hops from Germany. These are hops that have been compressed (even more than the plugs) into a single 11 lb brick. They are then vacuum sealed in foil bags. The freshness is excellent. If you ever order German whole hops and receive a few pieces of highly compressed hops, you'll know they were chipped off an 11 lb brick! Not to worry though, they fluff right up when wet.

Whole vs. Pellet Hops

I don't want to get into the entire pellet vs. whole hop debate right here (it'll actually be spread out amongst the later chapters as the relevant issues arise), but I do want to take this opportunity to point out the differences in how whole and pellet hops behave *physically* in the brewing process.

Whole hops take up quite a bit more space than the other hop forms. Consequently, it's harder to keep them stored properly (which is as cold as possible). Unless you have a spare freezer, it's not very practical to keep large quantities of whole hops around the house. Most microbrewers use pellets for the same reason, but those that use whole hops can generally get away with keeping them in the same cold storage that they use for kegs and/or bottles of beer. The reason is that they will use hops at a much faster rate than a homebrewer. Usually they will use the hop broker as their main cold storage and have hops shipped to them as their local stock is depleted.

Whole hops also behave quite differently than pellets in the brewing process. When the boil is over, the spent hops need to be separated from the wort. Traditionally, this was done with a device known as a hop back. The hop back was simply a screen (either made from perforated metal or cloth) that the wort was poured through. The hop back was literally a strainer, and it held the hops back (see where the name comes from?) and allowed the clear wort to pass through. The hop back also served the purpose of filtering the trub from the wort, by virtue of the spent hops acting as a finer filter than the screen holding the hops.

Obviously, hop pellet particles will not be caught by such a screen. If a finer screen is used, the hop pellet particles clog the screen quickly, and wort cannot pass through either. So now we have actually created two problems: we can't effectively filter out the hop particles and we have no means for filtering out the trub. Both of these problems are solved on a commercial scale by a device known as a *whirlpool separator*. It works on the principle that if you create a whirlpool with the wort, the heavier trub and hop particles will be deposited in a nice pile in the center of the tank, and you can then draw the wort off from the side, leaving the trub and hop particles behind. While this works well on a commercial scale, duplicating this effect on the homebrewing scale is difficult to impossible. The reason is that the distance from the center to the edge of the tank is much greater in a big commercial tank than it is in a hombrewer's boiling kettle.

You should also be aware that in general, hop pellet particles sink rather than float. This is a useful fact for homebrewers in removing the pellet particles from the wort. If your boiling kettle has a drain in it, all you need to do is let the wort settle so that most of the hop particles (and trub) sink below the level of the drain before you draw the wort from the kettle. You can also use an intermediate settling tank (like your bottling bucket) to accomplish the same thing. If you siphon the wort out of your kettle, let the wort settle and then set the siphon tube above the settled layer (this is actually harder than it sounds because you can't see through the side of your brew kettle).

If you use whole hops, you can simply pour the wort through a large strainer or colander, and this will catch most of the trub along with the hops. If your boiling kettle has a drain installed, you can also build the "strainer" into the drain by covering the interior end of the drain with a "chore boy" which is a common name (actually a brand name) of those stainless steel (or copper) wire "loopy" pot scrubbers, or use a tube of stainless steel screen with one end attached to the drain and the other end closed (just bend it over). If you siphon the wort out of your kettle, you just attach the pot scrubber to the end of your siphon tube.

So what's the point? The point is that your individual brewing equipment and practices should dictate whether or not you use pellets or whole hops. You cannot effectively use one form if your equipment or technique favors the other. If your equipment and technique is flexible enough to handle both, then you have the freedom to use pellets or whole hops (or both) at your choosing.

Hop Extracts and Oils

What follows is a brief description of the hop extract products on the market. Information on how to use these products in your beers will be presented in the appropriate places later in the book.

As you surely know by now, the "goods" in the hop are basically the alpha acids and essential oils. For the better part of the century, hop processors have been making extracts of hops in an effort to make the brewing process either more predictable or more economical, with varying degrees of success. This has led to a variety of products being offered to brewers throughout the years, all based on some kind of extract of the hop. Some of these are designed only to add bitterness to beer, others to enhance only the aroma, and some claiming to do both. These three categories of extracts are more sharply defined as: Iso-alpha extracts, Hop Oil extracts, and total extracts consisting of all of the hop constituents (including alphas and oils).

The extraction process has been carried out over the years in a variety of ways. Solvent extraction has been used for all three types of extract, but is most commonly used to extract alpha acids and for total extractions. Steam distillation has been used to extract the hop oils, either directly from the hops or from a solvent-extracted total extract.

The solvents used in the solvent-extraction process have been pretty nasty chemicals. The most common in recent and current use are either methylene chloride or hexane, two highly toxic chemicals. There was some hope quite a few years ago for an ethanol extract, but it didn't pan out. Recently, CO_2 has been used as the extracting solvent, and this has met with great success. There are two types of CO_2 extraction processes. The super-critical process uses high temperature, high pressure CO_2 and tends to extract everything from the hops. If you want to use a total extract, this is fine (except the heat involved changes the aroma profile of the oils). If you want just alphas or oils, the total extract needs to be further extracted. To get alphas, they use hexane. To get oils, they steam distill the extract. (If you're asking "What's the point of the CO_2 if they use solvents and heat anyway?" it's because it is more efficient and the next process I'm about to describe is patented.) The other type of CO_2 extraction process is the sub-critical process and it uses low temperature, low pressure liquid CO_2. It is selective for alpha and beta acids and hop oils. The hops oils are separated by a low temperature, vacuum distillation process. Since low heat is involved, no aroma changes occur.

The point of all this is that you want to make sure if you're buying hop extracts and oils, that you try and avoid those produced with toxic solvents, and for best aroma, those with minimal heat. It kind of all boils down to low temperature liquid CO_2 extraction.

Iso-Alpha Acid Extracts

Iso-alpha acid extracts are used to add bitterness to beer. They will not add any hop flavor, character or aroma. To get maximum efficiency, they are best used at the very end of the process. If added to the wort, they will be subject to the same fermentation losses as iso-alpha acids from the hops. If added after fermentation, almost all of the added iso-alpha acids remain in the beer. There are also side benefits to boiling your wort with real hops, so it is not advisable to use iso-alpha extract to bitter your beer entirely. There are some iso-alpha extracts sold to commercial brewers that have been chemically altered so they are not sensitive to light, which normally can cause a "sun-struck" or "skunky" flavor in the beer. Miller uses these extracts to bitter its normal beers so they can be packaged in clear bottles. These extracts are not normally available to the homebrewer.

I have seen some iso-alpha extracts on the market that give the brewer no clue as to strength. These are really worthless as you have no idea how bitter you are making your beer. Some are sold simply as a percentage iso-alpha acid (such as 30%) and leave it to the brewer to figure out how that relates to IBUs. And some go as far as to calibrate the product directly in IBUs/gallon.

Even though I have stated that it is not advisable to bitter your beer entirely with iso-alpha extracts, they do have many uses. The biggest asset they bring to the home and microbrewer is for use in correcting an under-bittered beer. If you have an extract that is calibrated in IBUs, it is also useful as a way of determining a beer's bitterness without the need for expensive lab equipment. This procedure is detailed in the chapter *All About Bittering*.

Although iso-alpha extracts that are made with toxic solvent extraction have been in use for many years, there are concerns that some of the solvent remains. (There is no issue with the heat used to remove the solvent as there is with hop oils.) Since low temperature CO_2 extracted products are available, I would advise that the brewer use these if possible.

Hop Oils

Hop oils have been on the market for many years. Adding hop oil to your beer will give it hop aroma and will not impart any bitterness. They are primarily used to simulate the effect of dry hopping by adding the hop oil at bottling or kegging. Some breweries in England use hop oil in the cask instead of real hops in order to get a more consistent product. Recently, some of the hop oils have been separated into fractions that are thought to be responsible for the late hop character in the beer, and these have been offered to home and microbrewers. One could also add hop oil at the end of the boil to get a late hop character (as opposed to a dry hop aroma), but this has only met with limited success. Taste panels all preferred the beers that were late-hopped with real hops.

Hop oils can be derived all from a single hop variety, or produced from a blend of varieties. Hop oils are blended so that a consistent product can be produced from year to year and batch to batch. This is especially important to commercial breweries, who want to make a very consistent beer. The disadvantage of the blends is that they don't resemble a specific hop aroma profile. Hop oils made only from one variety (say East Kent Goldings) are also available, but the selection is disappointingly small. Hopefully, if hop oils become more popular, this will change.

The pure oils are very difficult for the average homebrewer and microbrewer to use because they are so concentrated (typical usage rates are between 1 and 3 ppm in the beer). A tiny drop of pure hop oil is enough for many 5 gallon batches! To measure out such tiny amounts accurately requires micro-fine syringes or pipettes and the difficulty of adequately dispersing such a small amount into the beer has limited the success of the oils. Recently, formulated hop oils that are easy to disperse and measure have come on the market and so solves the problem. (This formulation is different than the varietal blending described above - a varietal blend would be subsequently formulated.)

The idea behind these formulated oils is that the oil is diluted in a carrier medium that makes it easy to measure. The problem is that oil really isn't very soluble in anything. The oil is really only suspended in the medium. The most common medium has been ethanol, but this has several problems. Only some of the oil's compounds are soluble in the ethanol. What doesn't dissolve becomes polymerized after a few days, which means that the molecules get bound together is such a way that they are no longer able to be redispersed in the oil and can no longer flavor the beer. And after some contact time, the ethanol changes the hop oil's methyl compounds to ethyl compounds, and these no longer have the same aroma. When ethanol is used as a temporary dispersant (the pure hop oil is mixed with the ethanol and immediately dosed into the beer), the polymerization and compound conversions are not a problem, but the measurement problem remains. Another issue with the ethanol-based formulations is that technically it's not legal to add alcohol to beer even in the small quantities we're taking about. This doesn't apply to homebrewers, but it is an issue for microbrewers.

The solution to this problem has been to create water-based formulations. We all know that oil won't dissolve in water, but it is possible to cause the oil to remain in suspension. Technically this is called an emulsion. Over the years, many attempts to emulsify hop oil have been made, and none has been quite successful because the emulsions have not been stable. After a few days to months, the hop oil separates again and it must be discarded. Recently, hop oils with permanently stable emulsions have been released, and these have been approved by the BATF for use in commercial beer. Other hop oil emulsions have started to appear on the market as well, but the reader is advised to ask about their stability and shelf life.

Another issue with hop oil formulations (ethanol or water based) is that of calibration. One can assume that if you buy a particular product that is not calibrated (say in ppm of hop oil) that it will be consistent from batch to batch. But this remains only an assumption. The recommendation is to buy a calibrated product.

Late Hop Essences

Research into which of the oil's compounds caused late hop character in beer (as opposed to a fresh hop aroma) has led to products called *late hop essences*. These are just the compounds from the oil that are supposedly responsible for a late hop character, and they happen to be soluble in ethanol and water. Two different late hop effects were identified by the research, each caused by a different "fraction" of the oil. They were identified as the "spicy" and "floral" fractions. The amount needed of these compounds is very small, on the order of 50-150 parts per billion in beer! Luckily since these are water and ethanol soluble, they can be easily diluted for more precise measurements.

The spicy fraction, in addition to adding a spicy character to the beer, is primarily responsible for the beer's mouthfeel. It adds a surprising amount of body to the beer. (Before using the spicy fraction, I thought all of a beer's body came only from the malt. Now I realize that hops play an important role in the perception of the beer's body.) The floral fraction adds a subtle floral *taste* to the beer (not a floral aroma). The spicy and late hop essences are sold separately, and the brewer can adjust the proportions of each to get the desired effect.

As with the hop oils and iso-alpha extracts, I will again repeat the suggestion to buy a calibrated product.

Chapter 6 - Buying and Evaluating Hops

In this chapter, we're going to talk about how to evaluate hops, the importance of proper hop packaging and storage, and give you some general guidelines for purchasing aroma and bittering hops. Armed with this knowledge, you'll be able to make better decisions about which hops to buy and who to buy them from.

Evaluating Hops

You have two very sensitive instruments to use in evaluating hops for purchase: your eyes and your nose! The first thing to do is make a visual inspection of the hops. Are they green or brown? Hops should definitely be green. They will usually have a few brown spots here and there, and maybe even a brown cone or two. This is not a problem as this browning probably occurred in the field (not every hop cone can be expected to be ripe at the same time). But if the entire batch is brown, forget it! The shade of green varies with variety and to some extent with the way they are dried. Don't assume that dark green is better than light green, or that a light green color means the hops are about to turn brown. Of course these comments apply mainly to whole hops. Pellets should also be green, and while it is rare to find pellets that have been so badly mistreated that they are now brown, I have seen them offered for sale. Don't buy them! Pellets should be mostly intact, but there may be some powder. If there is quite a bit of powder (which usually happens near the end of the big bag the pellets came from the hop broker in), then you need to be especially concerned with the packaging. Hop powder deteriorates the fastest of any hop product. If the powdery pellets are in good packaging (described a bit further on) then you need not worry. Otherwise, pick a different package. (When you open the package, use the powder first, if you're not going to use the whole package.)

For whole hops, get an impression of how well the cones have stayed intact. You should never expect to find all 100% intact cones, but they should at least be abundant. I can't give you an exact percentage of whole cones vs. broken cones, but you shouldn't have to go searching for an intact cone. If you do, or if there are none, this indicates rough handling of the hops and you should approach them with caution. It doesn't mean they need to be rejected, but it is a negative tick.

Next you should smell the hops. How they smell is dependent on the variety, but they should not smell stale. Really fresh hops should have a crisp, "piney" smell, but this can vary a good deal depending on the variety. Stale hops smell "cheesy" and some describe the odor as smelling like dirty gym socks.

If you are evaluating whole hops, smell them first as is. Next, take a cone and separate some of the bracteoles (petals) from the strig to expose the lupulin glands. These look like very fine yellow dust or pollen. Get some of the lupulin and rub it between your thumb and forefinger to crush the glands and release the resin. Your thumb and forefinger should immediately feel sticky. Smell your fingers immediately. You should have nice strong hop aroma. This is the aroma you will get if you dry hop with these hops. Now wait a few minutes and smell your fingers again. The hop aroma should still be present, but it should be milder. This is more like the aroma you will get from late hop additions.

For pellets, smell them as is. You will get some aroma, but it will usually not be very intense, especially if the hops are cold. Next, take a pellet (a small one) and break it apart. This is not very easy to do, especially between your fingers. The best way is to crush the pellet with something. If you're at home, put the pellet in a baggie and roll over it with a rolling pin or hit it with a wooden mallet, or just improvise on your own. If you're in a store, you'll have to figure out a way to do this. Have the store personnel help you. Now proceed as you would with whole hops: smell the powder, rub it between your fingers (which should get sticky) and smell again. Wait a few minutes and smell once more. (Now you can wash your hands.)

If the hops have passed the test so far, you will be assured they won't contribute any off-aromas to your beer. For whole hops, you may want to take the trouble to evaluate the bag for the amount of apparent stem and leaf material. Some stems and a few leaf parts are normal. Hops from Europe tend to have a higher stem content than domestic hops, especially East Kent Goldings. But if you are lucky enough to find East Kent Goldings in otherwise good shape, don't worry about the extra stems. Most domestic hops will be fairly free of seeds, but English hops (especially Fuggle) may have a fairly high seed content. This comes with the territory, and there really isn't a lot you can do about it. You don't really need to worry about other stuff in the hops (like aphids etc.) because the hop broker (or the state agriculture departments) should have rejected these hops well before the hops hit the market.

All this discussion assumes you have access to the hops. In your typical homebrew shop, the hops will be (should be!) all nicely sealed in proper packaging. This alone is a good indicator of the hops' quality. It won't hurt to ask if the dealer will open up a bag for you. If you're going to brew right away, go ahead and take that bag home (if the hops are in good shape). If your brewing is more than a month away, tell the dealer you'd like to open a bag to evaluate the hops, but you need to purchase a sealed bag. If the dealer does his own packaging, he may be able to properly reseal the bag for you before you leave. If not, he may be reluctant to open one and sell you another, and that's understandable. About the only thing you can do is take a chance on some hops and perform the evaluation when you get home. If they're really nasty, take them back and shop elsewhere for hops next time.

Hop Packaging and Storage

The previous section hinted that there were proper (and therefore improper) ways to package and store hops. We're going to address this topic in great detail later on (it gets its own chapter) but I want to give you some brief pointers about packaging and storage as they relate to buying hops, mainly from a retail store.

Hops lose their alpha acids and oils over time due to oxidation. Three things can be done to slow the process: refrigeration, anaerobic (free from air) packaging and keeping them out of the light. Of these three, refrigeration is the most important, followed by anaerobic (usually called barrier) packaging and lastly by light. The homebrew shop should at least be keeping their hops in a refrigerator. Even better would be a freezer. The colder they keep the hops, the better. If the hops are sitting out at room temperature, I advise you to buy your hops elsewhere. The hops should be packaged in barrier bags that are either vacuum packed or flushed with an inert gas such as nitrogen or CO_2. Your nose will tell you right away if the hops are in barrier bags. If you open the refrigerator door and the hop smell hits you in the face, it's coming right through the bags (this is assuming there isn't an open bag of hops or two in there for showing customers). If you have any doubt, take a package out of the fridge and wander around the store with it for a while. Take it to a far corner and smell the bag. If you smell the hops right through the bag, then it is not barrier material. Some barrier bags are opaque (the best bags, actually) so they will keep out the light (some do a better job than others). But most are clear, and most dealer's refrigerators are the kind with lights in them for displaying products. The lights may be great for attracting you to the hops, but they are not good for the hops. Usually these are big fluorescent tubes, positioned just inches away from the bags. This is bad news. Talk to your dealer and tell him that you really wouldn't mind if the hop fridge was dark (in fact you'd appreciate it). Anyway, pick a bag from the back if you can.

Buying Hops Mail Order

With all the concern over temperature, what if you need to (or want to) buy your hops from a mail order supplier? There can be many good reasons to buy your hops this way. You can choose a supplier that specializes in hops. You are likely to get a better selection and usually a better cared for product. And you will usually get a better price, even taking shipping into account. But the hops can get pretty warm while they are in transit. In the winter, they may actually stay very cold most of the time. But in the summer, a UPS truck can get over 100 degrees inside. This is not very good for the hops. If the hop supplier offers a reasonably priced "quick shipping" option, I advise you to take advantage of it, especially in the summer. If not, I wouldn't worry all that much. A few warm days won't make that much difference, and after all, the hops were shipped to your local dealer the same way.

Why Am I Buying "Last Year's" Hops?

Hops are harvested once a year, and they start showing up in homebrew shops in the last few months of the year in which they were harvested. For example, hops harvested in 1993 (called the '93 Crop) will show up near the end of 1993 and will be sold until the end of 1994 (or maybe even beyond). So crop years always seem a year out of date. This brings up the point that hops should be marked for the crop year. If they are not, you don't really know their age.

Hops from Europe can take considerably longer to show up here. They will start to arrive in late December and continue to trickle in until April or later.

Buying Bittering Hops

When buying hops that you're going to use for bittering (they can be either bittering or aroma hops) the most important aspect is the alpha acid content. The big brewers will pick hops that have higher alpha acid contents because it lowers their production costs. On the homebrew (and even the microbrew) scale, this should not be a deciding factor in choosing bittering hops. The difference will only amount to pennies a glass (if that much). The quality and brewing characteristics of the hops should govern your choice. But all else being equal, if the same variety hops from one supplier have a higher alpha acid content than another, it *may* be a reflection of the better handling by that supplier. Or it may simply be differences in grower or lot. Also, the highest alpha hops are not always what you want. If you want the hop signature of the bittering hop to come through in the beer, you'd want a hop with lower alphas. This allows you to use more hops to get a stronger hop signature.

These days, almost all hops are sold with an alpha acid rating. If they are not, STOP! Don't buy these hops. The rating may be on the package, or the ratings may be posted on the door of the fridge. In either case, you need to be concerned about the accuracy of the rating. This is important to get consistent, repeatable and predictable results in bittering your beer.

You need to ask about the source of the rating. Usually the alpha acid ratings are done by the hop broker and supplied with the hops. If the ratings are posted on the fridge, you can get some clues by looking at the piece of paper. If the paper lists a "range" for the alpha, then it is no better than the varietal guides in this book. Try and judge the age of the paper. Is it dated? Does it specifically reflect the current year's crop? Or is it brown and dusty and look like it's been there for 5 years? If this is the best data the store's got on the hops, then it is really the same as having no data at all.

In the next chapter, we'll tell you how to correct for any alpha losses that can occur during storage, and if the dealer is forthcoming about where the ratings and hops came from and how they've been stored since they were rated, you can estimate any losses that may have occurred since the hops were rated.

Buying Aroma Hops

With hops used for aroma (and not for bittering) you really don't care much about the alpha rating because the amount of bittering they will provide to your brew will be negligible. In this case we care only about the aroma. The aroma comes from the hop oils, and there is a trend in the industry to rate hops for oil content as well as alpha acid content.

If you can get aroma hops rated for oil content you are way ahead of the game. This will help you get more consistent aroma results in your beer. You are more likely to find oil content rated hops from mail order suppliers that specialize in hops, but eventually the stores will hopefully be providing this information just as they are providing alpha ratings now.

I have said that the hop aroma comes from the oils. While this is true, some of the aroma comes directly from the oils and some comes from the oxidation products of the oils. This is especially true of the noble varieties or those aroma characteristics we associate with "nobleness". So some aroma hops are actually better when there has been some aging, compared to when they are newly harvested. The domestic varieties Crystal, Liberty, Mt. Hood, Fuggle and Willamette would fall into this category. Imported hops like Czech Saaz and East Kent Goldings are already pretty well aged by the time we get them.

When buying aroma hops, use your nose. Anything that smells bad to you will end up in your beer. Don't buy a hop because it's in a recipe if it doesn't smell good to you. Use the guides in this book to pick a substitute.

This is especially true if you're dry hopping. For dry hopping, you usually want the absolute freshest hops available.

Choosing a Hop Supplier

If you've read the rest of this chapter, you should be in a good position to choose a hop supplier. The following check list can be used to rate your choice of supplier. You

can apply your own weighting to the items, but the best
hop supplier should get all "yes" answers.

Hop Supplier Check List

__ Wide variety of hops available in the form I use?
__ Use barrier packaging with inert gas/vacuum packing?
__ Use foil/mylar bags (better than clear barrier bags)?
__ Use cold storage (the colder the better)?
__ No bright lights in the cooler? (Doesn't matter if the
   packaging is light-tight)
__ Accurate alpha acid ratings?
__ Are the packages marked with crop year?
__ Oil content ratings?
__ Good return policy?
__ If mail order, a reasonable "quick ship" option?
__ Good prices?

Chapter 7 - Storing Hops

Hops are only harvested once per year, and yet we must brew with them for the entire year or longer. So it makes sense to keep them as fresh as possible until the next year's crop is available. In this chapter we're going to talk about everything related to storing your hops so they remain as fresh as possible. We will give you a method for estimating alpha acid losses over time under various storage conditions.

Hops have three main ingredients that brewers care about: the alpha acids, the beta acids and the essential oils. Normally we concern ourselves with only two of the three: the alpha acids and the oils. All three of these components undergo changes as the hops age.

Hop Deterioration

Hops start to lose their alpha acids and oils as soon as they are harvested. The rate of loss is dependent on the storage temperature, the amount of air present and the hop variety. Basically, the lower the temperature, the less the hops deteriorate. It has been shown that the rate of deterioration is halved for every 15°C drop in temperature. Oxygen also causes the alpha acids to oxidize and some of the oxidation components are responsible for the "cheesy" aroma of old hops. The oxidized alpha acids cannot be isomerized and are not nearly as bitter as iso-alpha acids. So oxygen is definitely bad for alpha acids. The beta acids do form bitter compounds when they are oxidized, so some believe that this makes up for the loss of alpha acids. In fact, it has been argued that cold storage and anaerobic conditions are not necessary for bittering hops, as long as the boil is long enough and open enough to allow the cheesy aroma to escape. But brewers aren't buying the argument (who can blame them?). Taste tests have also proven that there is a distinct difference in the quality of the beers made with stale hops.

The variety of the hop also plays a major role in storage. Hops are usually classified as "kettle" or "bittering" hops and "aroma" hops. Bittering hops have a higher alpha acid content than aroma hops and their storage characteristics are more important. Under the same storage conditions, certain varieties will lose more alpha acids than others. Each hop variety has a differing amount of natural antioxidants present, and some variety's lupulin glands are more permeable to air than others. One common test for the "storageability" of the hops is done by measuring the amount of alpha and beta acids lost over a 6 month period at 20°C (68°F). There is a direct relationship between the losses and the Hop Storage Index (HSI). The HSI is a number obtained by spectrophotometric determinations of the alpha and beta acids. If you know the HSI and/or the % Lost figures for a particular variety and the present alpha acids content, you can estimate the original alpha acids or future alpha acids content. Formulas for predicting the alpha acid losses will be presented later in the chapter.

The oils also deteriorate and oxidize over time. But it is believed that some oxidation of the oils is beneficial to the hop aroma. Not enough research has been done in the area of characterizing the oil content loss rates for various varieties, so we are not able to predict oil losses accurately at this time. One could make the assumption that the rate of oil loss is directly related to the loss of alpha acids and use the alpha acid loss formulas to predict the oil losses as well. But again, due to the lack of experimental data to back this up, it remains only an assumption.

It should also be mentioned that exposure to light hastens the deterioration as well. At home, this is not much of an issue because most freezers are dark inside. But in your local homebrew store, a "display" freezer may have fluorescent lights in it. While this certainly makes the hop display more attractive to your eye, the hops would be better served if the light was removed.

Hop Storage

For optimum preservation of hops' valued qualities, they should be stored as cold as possible (30 to -5°F) and away from air. The compression of the hops into bales, pellets and plugs helps keep all but the surface layers away from air. Even so, air still penetrates and causes some oxidation. The cold temperature slows the oxidation process. As was mentioned earlier, some hop varieties don't store as well as others. At some point in the season, hop brokers will take all remaining unsold bales of poor storing hops and turn them into pellets. The pellets don't really keep out much more oxygen, but most importantly they take up so little space they can now be vacuum packed to slow the deterioration.

The reason pellets are so prevalent in the homebrewing trade is that they *appear* to deteriorate more slowly than whole hops when stored in less than ideal conditions. The reason for this is they take up much less storage space, making it much more practical to keep them cold. And microbrewers like them for an additional reason: they are easy to remove from the wort if the brewery uses a whirlpool separator. However, if whole hops are stored and packaged properly, they will last just as long as pellets.

Whole hops compressed in their 200 lb burlap-wrapped bales are stored in huge cold storage facilities operated by the hop brokers. The cold temperature and compression helps minimize storage losses. Photo courtesy of Hopunion USA, Inc.

Compression of the whole hops into bales slows the oxidation because it's harder for the oxygen to get at the hops. But when the bale is broken up to be portioned into homebrewer sized quantities, the compression is lost. Now air can get at the hops much more easily. Because of the compression and therefore the space savings, hop plugs can be a good compromise between the convenience of pellets and the advantages of whole hops, assuming the plugs are fresh and of high quality to begin with.

Hop Packaging for Sale to the Homebrewer

Vacuum packing or inert gas packaging in an oxygen

barrier material is the best. The common type of oxygen barrier packaging is the "boiling bag" which is clear and made from a lamination of two types of plastic: the inner layer is a food grade polyethylene (the same stuff zip lock bags are made from). Polyethylene is not a barrier material, but does make a good heat seal and is the main reason it's there. The outer layer is made from polyester (also known as mylar or nylon) and is what provides the oxygen barrier layer. The next step up in effectiveness is the aluminized mylar bag (also known as a foil bag or pouch) and this adds a layer of aluminum that increases the barrier protection over 10-fold. It also more than doubles the cost so it's not widely used even though it's better.

Some suppliers still insist on selling their hops in polyethylene bags. These provide almost no barrier protection. Hops that have been insufficiently protected offer dubious alpha acid values and should be approached with skepticism or not used at all. See the chapter on *Buying and Evaluating Hops* for more details.

To tell the barrier bags apart from simple polyethylene bags, I assume you know what a zip lock or sandwich bag feels like. These are polyethylene. You can smell the hops right through the bag (this should tell you something). They also have a slightly "frosted" appearance and are kind of "oily" looking, but not polished looking. The clear barrier bags are noticeably stiffer and thicker. They are also "shiny" and polished looking and not "frosted" like the polyethylene bags. The foil bags usually look either silver or gold.

Some resealable barrier bags are on the market. They seem to offer the advantage of barrier protection and being convenient to reseal. However, the bag suppliers I talked to stated that they can't get a perfect bond between the zipper and the bag, and pinholes are common along the seam. They are probably better than standard zip lock bags, but probably not by much.

Recently some "silvery-looking" bags have been used for hop packaging. These are nice and shiny and look at first glance to be the same as the aluminized mylar bags described above. *Beware!* These are really "anti-static" bags used by the electronics industry and are not food grade material! They do have some aluminum coating, but not enough to provide an oxygen barrier, only a static barrier. It is also not known if the plastic itself is a barrier material. The first clue about this bag is that you can kind of see the hops through it. The silver coating is translucent, not opaque and mirror-like. They are also usually tinted gray. I would approach any hops in this packaging with skepticism.

What To Do When You Get Them Home

First, if the hops are not packaged properly (and you had no choice but to buy them) you need to get them in suitable barrier packaging as soon as possible. However, if you're going to brew with them in the next few weeks or so and are going to use them all up, don't worry about it, just put them in the freezer for now. If the hops were packaged properly, don't open them until you need to. Store them in the freezer. Once you've opened them, the biggest problem is what to do with the remainder. If they came in a vacuum sealed or nitrogen flushed bag, the best thing to do is reseal the bag with a "home quality" vacuum sealer. These cost anywhere from $20 on sale to $100 depending on the seal width (and length) and the amount of heat they put out. Even the cheapest sealers will put out enough heat to seal the standard clear barrier bags. They will not unfortunately always put out enough heat to seal the aluminized bags. To find a sealer, look around in kitchen supply departments and stores, catalog showrooms and hardware stores. The best bet is to take an old piece of bag with you and see how it seals. You can always transfer the hops to the bags that come with the sealer, but beware that the bags supplied with some of the cheap sealers are not true barrier bags, but they're better than polyethylene. For replacement bags, I recommend the Dazey brand bags that were designed for the original "Seal-A-Meal" (not the ones for their vacuum sealer). They are true oxygen barrier bags.

If you keg or otherwise have CO_2 or nitrogen available, you can flush some mason jars with the gas, put in the hops and add a layer of gas and reseal the jar. Another alternative is PET plastic jars like the ones peanut butter comes in. Not only is PET a reasonable oxygen and moisture barrier, I like it because it won't break should you accidently drop the jar. I advise you to practice with the gas as it's very easy to blast your hops all over the room. And always use a gas regulator! If you can't do any of this, put the hops in a mason or PET jar, filling as full as possible, and put them in the freezer, it's better than nothing.

How Long Will They Last?

Well, like most things in brewing, the answer is "It depends." If you keep them very cold and free from oxygen hops should "last" a few years. It's not uncommon for hop brokers to be selling hops from 2 or 3 seasons ago that have been pelletized and vacuum sealed. And commercial breweries are still using last year's crop well into the current year's harvest. This is not to say that the oils and alpha acids will be exactly the same as when you purchased them, but the hops won't be "bad" (until they get below 50% of their original alpha acid value). This leads us to the next subject.

Predicting Alpha Acid Loss

Based on published research and the known storage properties of commonly used hops, it is possible to predict the alpha acid content of your hops at any given point in time. To be able to do this, you must know the following: hop variety and its associated storage properties, reasonably accurate alpha acid percentage for the hops when you bought them, storage conditions (aerobic or anaerobic), the storage temperature and the number of days from the date at which you knew the alpha acids to the date for which you are predicting them. To perform these calculations, you'll need a scientific calculator, a spreadsheet program or logarithm tables.

The hop storage properties are dependent on the variety and there are three ways of reporting the data, all based on the Hop Storage Index or the direct measurements mentioned earlier. The first and least common way is the actual HSI number. This is rarely encountered in the hop trade and is primarily used as an in-house reference at hop laboratories in research centers and large breweries. The hop brokers publish the storage qualities as either "percent alpha remaining" or "percent alpha lost" after 6 months of storage at 20°C. For our calculations we will use the latter, and simply call it % Lost. If you have the "percent remaining" figure, simply subtract it from 100 to get the % Lost.

Many uncertainties surround the accuracy of the alpha acids level shown on the packaging at the point of purchase. How were the hops handled since the rating was assigned? Fortunately, the packaging itself may tell a large part of the story - high quality packaging and care in storage reflects care and concern for the product and lends assurance that the labeled values are reliable. This is addressed in more detail in the chapter on *Buying and*

Evaluating Hops. In any case, ask your hop supplier how the hops were handled since they were rated. Then you can use these formulas to estimate the current alpha acids of the hops. You will most likely have to do two sets of calculations: one for the storage losses before you bought them based on the supplier's storage conditions, and a second for your own storage conditions.

The rest of the required data is readily available in your kitchen or brewery (I assume you know how you're storing the hops and at what temperature). Don't make any assumptions about how cold your freezer is. Get a "freezer thermometer" for a couple of bucks and measure it.

The "number of days from the date on which you knew the alpha acid percentage" business is probably the hardest thing to describe clearly. Basically, if you knew the alpha acid content on the day you bought the hops, this becomes day 1. If you bought the hops 1 month ago, it is now day 30. If you want to know what they will be one month from now, that will be day 60. And so on.

Step-by-step Instructions for Predicting Alpha Acid Losses

To make the math a bit easier, I've precalculated some of the values for you. All you need to do is look them up in a table. But for those that want to know all of the gory details, the formulas and procedures used to derive the table values are provided at the end of the chapter in the section called "Backup Math".

The first step is to look up the % Lost for the hop variety in Chapter 4. If the variety is newly released or otherwise not listed there, you'll need to obtain that figure from your hop supplier. Next we need to determine the

"Rate Constant" (which would normally be called *k* by our mathematical friends, so we'll call it that too) which is based on the % Lost. This rate is the constant used in the log expression to determine the curve of the loss vs. time. Find % Lost on Table 7-1 and next to it will be the value to use for *k*. Now find the Temperature Factor (TF) from Table 7-2, based on your storage temperature. From Table 7-3, find the Storage Factor (SF) based on how you will be storing hops. Lastly, determine the number of days from when you knew the alpha acid content to when you want to know the new alpha acid content, and we'll call this DAYS. The original alpha acid percentage when we bought the hops is

% Lost	k	% Lost	k	% Lost	k
10%	0.00059	27%	0.00175	44%	0.00322
11%	0.00065	28%	0.00183	45%	0.00332
12%	0.00071	29%	0.00190	46%	0.00342
13%	0.00077	30%	0.00198	47%	0.00353
14%	0.00084	31%	0.00206	48%	0.00363
15%	0.00090	32%	0.00214	49%	0.00374
16%	0.00097	33%	0.00222	50%	0.00385
17%	0.00104	34%	0.00231	51%	0.00396
18%	0.00110	35%	0.00239	52%	0.00408
19%	0.00117	36%	0.00248	53%	0.00419
20%	0.00124	37%	0.00257	54%	0.00431
21%	0.00131	38%	0.00266	55%	0.00444
22%	0.00138	39%	0.00275	56%	0.00456
23%	0.00145	40%	0.00284	57%	0.00469
24%	0.00152	41%	0.00293	58%	0.00482
25%	0.00160	42%	0.00303	59%	0.00495
26%	0.00167	43%	0.00312	60%	0.00509

Table 7-1   Use to find k for % Lost Values

Temp C	Temp F	TF	Temp C	Temp F	TF	Temp C	Temp F	TF
20	68	1.000	3	37.4	0.456	-14	6.8	0.208
19	66.2	0.955	2	35.6	0.435	-15	5	0.198
18	64.4	0.912	1	33.8	0.416	-16	3.2	0.189
17	62.6	0.871	0	32	0.397	-17	1.4	0.181
16	60.8	0.831	-1	30.2	0.379	-18	-0.4	0.173
15	59	0.794	-2	28.4	0.362	-19	-2.2	0.165
14	57.2	0.758	-3	26.6	0.345	-20	-4	0.157
13	55.4	0.724	-4	24.8	0.330	-21	-5.8	0.150
12	53.6	0.691	-5	23	0.315	-22	-7.6	0.144
11	51.8	0.660	-6	21.2	0.301	-23	-9.4	0.137
10	50	0.630	-7	19.4	0.287	-24	-11.2	0.131
9	48.2	0.602	-8	17.6	0.274	-25	-13	0.125
8	46.4	0.574	-9	15.8	0.262	-26	-14.8	0.119
7	44.6	0.548	-10	14	0.250	-27	-16.6	0.114
6	42.8	0.524	-11	12.2	0.239	-28	-18.4	0.109
5	41	0.500	-12	10.4	0.228	-29	-20.2	0.104
4	39.2	0.477	-13	8.6	0.218	-30	-22	0.099

Table 7-2   Use to find Temperature Factor for Storage Temperature

Storage Conditions	SF
Not sealed or sealed in poly bags	1
Sealed in barrier packaging or airtight jars, but not free from oxygen	0.75
Sealed in barrier packaging or airtight jars under a vacuum or inert atmosphere such as nitrogen or carbon dioxide	0.5

Table 7-3. Use to find Storage Factor for Storage Conditions

113

called A_o (for alpha/original) and the future alpha acid value is A_f (for alpha/future).

Now use the following formula:

$$A_f = A_o * (1 / e^{(k*TF*SF*DAYS)})$$

where e is the base of the natural logarithm. Note to spreadsheet users: e raised to a power is usually expressed as EXP(n). Scientific calculators will usually have an $e^{(x)}$ key.

Let's walk through an example. Let's say we bought some Cascade at 6.4% alpha acid one month ago and we want to brew with it one week from today. We're storing it in our home freezer which is around $10°F$ in its original nitrogen flushed oxygen barrier packaging. We look up Cascade and find its % Lost value is 50%. Looking in Table 7-1, we see that a % Lost of 50% gives us the value for k as 0.00385. From Table 7-2, our value for TF is 0.228, and from Table 7-3 the value for SF is 0.5. The value for DAYS is 37, since we bought the hops 30 days ago and we're brewing 7 days from now (30 + 7 − 37).

So our formula now looks like:

$$A_f = 6.4 * (1 / e^{(0.00385*0.228*0.5*37)})$$

which gives us 6.3% (rounded) which really isn't all that much different than the original value of 6.4%, but it proves that good storage conditions can really make a difference in a poor storing hop like Cascade. Now if we stored it at room temperature in a poly bag the numbers would look like:

$$A_f = 6.4 * (1 / e^{(.00385*1*1*37)})$$

which equals 5.6% alpha, and that is a much more significant difference! It also shows the effect of poor storage conditions.

Summary

The hop variety, storage temperature and storage conditions all play a role in determining how fast alpha acids are lost from the hops. Of these, temperature is the most important factor that we have control over. Next is the hop variety and finally the aerobic or anaerobic storage conditions.

Chart 7-1 compares aerobic and anaerobic storage of Eroica and Galena - two high alpha varieties with different storage properties and for two different storage temperatures. As you can see, if you have choice it makes sense to choose a hop that has good storage properties vs. poor and you can also see the dramatic effect that temperature has. Now you don't always have a choice - Cascade is Cascade and there's nothing you can do about it. But if you're looking for a general purpose bittering hop, Cluster, Perle or Galena are better choices than Chinook or Eroica (but most of the *really* poor storing bittering hops have faded from the market, such as Olympic and Comet, and I haven't even included them in the book for that reason). To see the effect that temperature has on a poor storing variety, Chart 7-2 compares Cascade stored at +20°C and -20°C in unsealed storage.

Now that you know the effect that proper storage has on hops, you are in a much better position to pick a hop supplier that will give you a fresher product. You can consider their packaging and storage temperature. You can also take advantage of closeout sales on last season's hops if you know the hops have been properly stored.

Finally, to get better and more consistent results when bittering your beer, you now have a tool to calculate and predict what the alpha acid percentages will be for any given point in time, based on your storage conditions.

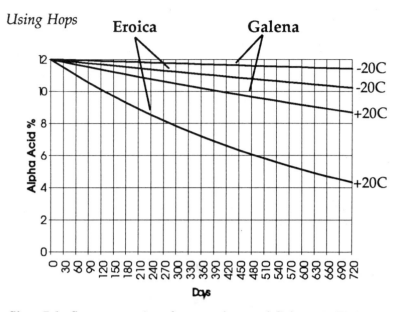

Chart 7-1 *Contrasts projected storage losses of Galena vs. Eroica at +20 and -20°C. Assumes both start at 12% alpha and sealed, inert storage. Plot is based on theoretical data and plotted according to the formulas presented in this chapter.*

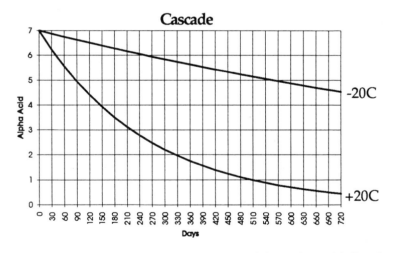

Chart 7-2. *Contrasts projected storage losses of Cascade at +20°C and -20°C, in unsealed storage. Plot is based on theoretical data and plotted according to the formulas presented in this chapter.*

Backup Math

The % Lost number comes from the Hop Storage Index or is measured directly. The data is generally provided by the hop brokers and researchers and for most common varieties available today, it is listed in chapter 4. If you know the HSI for a variety, you can calculate the % Lost by using the following formula:

$$\% \text{ Lost} = \log(\text{HSI} / 0.25) * 110$$

where log is the base 10 logarithm.

The value for k (the rate constant) is calculated according to the following formula:

$$k = (\ln A_o - \ln A_n) / 180$$

where ln is the natural logarithm, A_o is the original alpha acid value and A_n is the new alpha acid value after 180 days. Now you may ask, "How do I get the original alpha and new alpha values?" Well it turns out that you don't need to know them. If you know the % Lost you can calculate A_o and you can assume any arbitrary number for A_n. Calculate A_o (for any value of A_n) using the following formula:

$$A_o = (A_n * 100) / (100 * \% \text{ Lost})$$

The reason A_n can be any arbitrary number is that all we are really calculating here is a ratio, based on % Lost. Just make sure that when you go back to the k calculation you use the same arbitrary number for A_n that you used to calculate A_o.

The temperature factor (TF) is based on the research that showed the rate of deterioration is halved for every 15°C drop in temperature. This is an exponential curve and I simply used Excel's "curve fit" algorithms to fill in the data points, using 20°C (68°F) as the point at which no

117

adjustment is necessary (because this is where the data is measured and needs no adjustment). What I have not done is calculate a temperature factor for values above 20°C (values >1) because the table was getting fairly large and you really shouldn't be storing your hops anywhere near this temperature anyway!

The Storage Factor (SF) is based on interpretations of published research on hop storage. A factor of 1 means no adjustment, again correlating with the measurements of % Lost. The factor 0.5 was derived experimentally by the researchers. The factor of 0.75 is the estimated median value for the median storage method.

Chapter 8 - All About Bittering

The primary purpose of hops is to add bitterness to beer. This chapter will address all of the details about how hops add bitterness to your beer, and how you can predict and measure the bitterness in your beer. We're going to cover a lot of ground in this chapter, so let's get to it.

How Hops Bitter the Beer

There are likely thousands of compounds in hops, many of which have yet to be discovered, but there are only a handful that have any interest to the brewer when it comes to bittering. These compounds are the *alpha acids*. The three main alpha acids are *humulone, adhumulone* and *cohumulone*. Of these, humulone is the most often studied and is also the most abundant. Cohumulone is the subject of much controversy among brewers and hop researchers. There is a widely held belief that hops with high levels of cohumulone have a harsher bitter character than hops with low cohumulone levels. No conclusive proof has been offered one way or the other. Adhumulone is hardly ever discussed, and occurs in minor amounts compared to the other two alpha acids.

Alpha acids are bitter. There is only one problem.

They are not very soluble in water and they are even less soluble in beer. In order for the alpha acids to add bitterness to the beer, they need to be converted into a form that can be dissolved in beer. Luckily for us, this happens in wort boiling through a process known as *isomerization*. That's a fancy word that means the alpha acid molecules are rearranged, without adding or subtracting anything from them. The resulting compounds are called *iso-alpha acids*, and often just *iso-alphas* or simply *isos*. Iso-alpha acids are about as bitter as the alpha acids, but they dissolve much better in beer. We'll discuss isomerization in greater detail later in the chapter.

The *beta acids* are also the subject of much debate among brewers and hop researchers. The beta acids (*lupulone, colupulone* and *adlupulone*) are only marginally bitter and even less soluble in water and beer. They don't isomerize in normal wort boiling. However, when the beta acids are oxidized, which happens in storage and to some extent in wort boiling, bitter compounds do result. Some researchers have postulated that oxidized beta acids pick up where alpha acids leave off in old hops (the oxidized alpha acids aren't very bitter) since old hops impart more bitterness to beer than would seem possible based on their alpha acid contents. While this may work in the lab, taste testers reject beer that has been brewed with these old hops. We will assume, therefore, that the beta acids' contribution to the beer's bitterness is negligible to non-existent and won't concern ourselves with them any more.

Quantifying Bitterness

Just how bitter is a beer? In order to describe the intensity of a beer's bitterness, we need a common language that we all understand and agree upon. Historically, a beer's bitterness used to be described in terms of the hopping rate, usually given as a measurement in pounds of hops per barrel of beer, or even worse (but more common), in pounds of hops per quarter of malt (a quarter of malt equals 336 lbs). Many years ago, the professional brewing community decided that a better way of discussing the bitterness of the beer was required. But the Americans and the Europeans couldn't agree on the measurement method, so for some time they each had their own bittering unit. Today all the differences have been resolved and there is now a standard world-wide unit that is used to describe the level of bitterness in beer. It is called the *International Bittering Unit* and is usually shortened to *IBU*, or sometimes just *BU*.

The IBU

It is important to understand the major improvement the IBU brings us in how we describe bitterness. The old way was to quantify the amount of hops (or alphas) that were used to make the beer. On the other hand, IBUs are a measurement of how much bitterness is in the finished beer. This is important if you realize that only a fraction of the alpha acids put into the wort show up as iso-alpha acids in the finished beer, and this fraction changes for every brewer (and for different beers made by the same brewer).

The IBU is roughly equivalent to milligrams per liter of iso-alpha acids appearing in the finished beer. So a beer with 25 IBUs would have approximately 25 mg of iso-alpha acids in each liter of beer. IBUs are most commonly measured by an instrument known as a spectrophotometer. A sample of beer is shaken with a solvent (iso-octane) which extracts the iso-alpha acids from the beer. The solvent/iso-alpha acids mixture is then put into the spectrophotometer, which measures the absorbance at a certain wavelength in the ultra-violet (UV) spectrum. The amount of light absorbed is proportional to the amount of iso-alpha acids in the sample and the IBU number is calculated based on the absorbance reading.

It would be nice if UV-spectrophotometers were affordable by home brewers, but they cost upwards of $5000 for a unit with enough precision to give accurate results. Even most microbreweries can't afford this luxury.

However, the future for low cost, easy to use iso-alpha acids measurement that the home or microbrewer can afford is not all that bleak. Your author is actively researching this area, but nothing is ready for release yet. In the meantime, later in this chapter I'll give you a practical method for estimating a beer's IBU rating and formulas that will allow you to predict the number of IBUs you'll get in the final beer.

AAUs and HBUs

Since IBUs were not easily measured by homebrewers, the first homebrewing texts proposed alternate methods of estimating a beer's bitterness. Since there was no practical way to measure the beer's *final* bitterness, they went back to the older methods of describing bitterness only in terms of the hop additions.

The *AAU* was first proposed by the late Dave Line, considered the father of modern homebrewing. AAU stands for *Alpha Acid Unit* and is the amount of alpha acids in 1 ounce of hops. For example, one ounce of hops that have 5% alpha acid content would be 5 AAUs. Two ounces of these hops would be 10 AAUs. A half ounce of these hops would be 2.5 AAUs.

The AAU is also known as the *HBU* or *Homebrew Bittering Unit*. This has been popularized by *Zymurgy* magazine and by Charlie Papazian in his popular *The New Complete Joy of Homebrewing* book and the AAU is used currently by popular author Dave Miller.

Both of these authors admit the shortcomings of the AAU/HBU. The AAU/HBU only describes the amount of alpha acids you put into your beer. AAUs/HBUs need to be tied to the volume of a given recipe - 5 HBUs/AAUs in 5 gallons will not give the same bitterness as 5 HBUs/AAUs in 10 gallons. But most importantly, they don't take alpha acid losses into account and this varies quite a bit with your brewing procedure. At best, AAUs are a simple shorthand way of expressing the amount of alpha acids used in a recipe. For example, a recipe could list hops as an ingredient by stating "2 ounces of Cascade at 5% alpha acid" or "10 HBUs/AAUs of Cascade." They can't, however, be used to describe the final beer's bitterness. It hardly seems worth the confusion. Admittedly the HBU/AAU and the fact that there are no complicated formulas to follow is attractive to beginning homebrewers. But the old saying "You get what you pay for," certainly applies here. I recommend a brewer take just a few more minutes to do a proper IBU calculation. It really isn't very hard, and not only will your beers be more consistent, you'll now have a internationally recognized way of describing their bitterness.

Hop Utilization

It would be great if the amount of alpha acid we put into the wort equaled the amount of iso-alpha acids that ended up in the finished beer. Even if losses occurred, it would be great if these losses were identical for every beer, every brewer and every brewery. Of course, life is not perfect. Losses of alpha acids do occur, and there are many factors that affect the amount of the loss.

The term used to describe the efficiency of the bittering process is called *hop utilization* or usually just the *utilization*. If we put 100 milligrams of alpha acids into the kettle for each liter of wort, and when we measure the IBUs of the final beer we get 25 IBUs (remembering that IBUs are roughly equal to mg/liter of iso-alpha acids), then our utilization is 25%. As a formula, utilization looks like:

$$\% \text{ Utilization} = \frac{\text{amount of iso-alpha acids present}}{\text{amount of alpha acids used}} * 100$$

It is very important to remember that utilization expresses the efficiency of alpha acid utilization as iso-alpha acids *in the finished beer*. Most homebrewers believe that what goes on in the boil is all that matters in calculating utilization, and so they make the mistake of equating the extraction and isomerization of alpha acids in the boil as utilization. *It is not!* It does have an impact on the final utilization, but it is not everything.

Factors Affecting Utilization

There are many factors that affect hop utilization. They are:

- Hop rate during boiling (the amount of alphas introduced into the wort)
- Hop form (whole, pellets or extracts, and whether the hops are bagged or not)
- Boil conditions (vigor and temperature)
- Boil time vs. hop introduction time
- Boil volume
- Wort gravity
- Hop rate during fermentation
- Wort pH
- Yeast growth and flocculation characteristics
- Filtration (if applicable)

Some of these interact with each other - for example, an artificially low boil volume (as is common with extract brewers who typically boil in a small volume and then dilute the wort with water prior to pitching) will have the effect of increasing both the hop rate and the wort gravity during the boil.

All of these factors can be divided into two groups: Things that happen during the boil and things that happen during fermentation. First we're going to discuss what happens during the boil.

When hops are added to boiling wort, the resins containing the alpha acids and the essential oils begin to be extracted from the lupulin glands. The oils are responsible for the aroma effects, and we'll discuss those in later chapters. Research has shown that this extraction happens very quickly, on the order of 10-15 minutes for whole hops, quicker for pellets because the lupulin glands have been burst. But alpha acids will only stay in solution at high temperatures. When the wort is cooled, most of the alpha acids will drop out of solution, and those that don't will be lost during fermentation. As the wort continues to boil, isomerization begins to take place. The rate of isomerization is dependent on the vigor of the boil (a vigorous boil is essential to efficient isomerization), the pH of the wort, the amount of alpha acids in the wort (hopping rate), the wort gravity during the boil, the volume of the boil vs. the final batch volume (which affects the hopping rate and boil gravity), the temperature of the boil and the presence of the inert hop material (ground or whole). If the hops are in a hop bag, the effect of having this inert material in the wort is greatly reduced, and isomerization will be less efficient. The longer the boil continues, the more isomerization takes place, up to a point where the reaction either reverses itself, or iso-alpha acids begin to be degraded. The point at which this happens (and exactly what happens) is still a subject of debate. Some researchers claim that this point is reached in about two hours, while some say it is four. Since most brewers only boil their wort for 60-90 minutes, it is not of much concern to us. It appears that the maximum amount of iso-alpha acids that can be isomerized is somewhere around 60-75%. Another 8-10% of the iso-alpha acids are adsorbed (meaning they cling to the surface of) the hot and cold breaks. This number appears to be fairly constant, even given wide variations in the amount of break, composition of the wort and the method and length of cooling. Any remaining non-isomerized alpha acids precipitate out upon wort cooling. About 10% of the alpha acids are unable to be accounted for, being either transformed into compounds that were not detected or otherwise being destroyed in the process. In the following formulas, the loss of iso-compounds on the trub and those we can't account for are already figured in, so we don't have to continually deal with them.

After the wort is cooled and aerated, the yeast is pitched and fermentation begins. Iso-alpha acids are adsorbed onto the yeast cell walls. The amount is dependent on two factors: The total growth of the yeast crop and the amount of time the yeast stays in suspension. Of these two, the latter is the more important. Research has shown that there can be around a 5% variation in the total utilization in beers fermented with slowly flocculating yeasts (which stay in suspension for a long time) and those of normal flocculation. It follows that fast flocculating yeasts would cause variation in the other direction. Most of the iso-alpha acids lost during fermentation are carried to the surface of the wort with the carbon dioxide generated during fermentation and are present in the "dirty head" that forms in the first stages of fermentation. If this dirty head is stirred back into the wort at the proper time, hop utilization is increased by some 18%. But what usually happens is that these iso-alpha acids are lost. In commercial practice, this head may be skimmed. On the homebrew level, it may be blown out if the brewer uses the "blow-off" method. Otherwise it is pushed to the sides of the fermenter where it sticks. Simultaneously the compounds harden up (apparently due to oxidation) and they are no longer soluble in the fermenting beer. So that which doesn't stick to the fermenter walls will fall back through the beer, but not be redissolved. So regardless of the fermentation method, these alpha acids are lost. Lastly, filtration of the beer will cause further losses of iso-alpha acids.

Predicting Utilization

Much has been written in the homebrew literature about how to predict utilization. Not much has been written in the commercial brewing literature on this subject. Why? Because they have the tools to measure their *actual* utilization, and after a few trial brews, they will know how to adjust their hopping rate to keep the same number of IBUs in their beer. They also have the luxury of being able to blend batches with varying bitterness levels to arrive at a consistent product (you didn't think each batch came out the same at even the megabreweries, did you?). They not only do this analytically with lab measurements, but confirm the results with taste panels. Homebrewers and smaller microbrewers, on the other hand, don't have these luxuries. I will present a method by which you can test your final product's bitterness with reasonable accuracy, so this will help you confirm your utilization, but homebrewers and microbrewers change their recipes and methods a lot more often than the big brewers, so it is useful to have decent predictive formulas as well.

The formulas presented in the homebrew literature to date have been fairly simple-minded. They take into account the boil time, and usually the gravity of the wort during boiling. I have modified the most popular of these formulas to take more of the brewing variables into account. I have done this in a manner that lets you "keep it simple" or get as complicated with the calculations as you like.

The Fine Print!

I would be remiss if I didn't mention here that *all* IBU prediction formulas, (no matter how many factors we try to account for) are subject to errors because we're really just making educated guesses as to what's going on with each brew. *So be prepared to make your own adjustments to the formulas if they don't seem to be working for you.* If the beer doesn't have the right amount of bitterness, most brewers will blame everything *but* the formula, when it is the formula itself that is at fault. Remember that just because it's math, that doesn't make it science! Also, if you want to use some of these correction factors, be aware of the fact they are new and still largely unproven. They were based on published research (see the references in the *Bibliography* section) and utilization data from a few batches where the IBUs were measured and the brewing variables were known, but I would have liked to have much more data. Research is continuing, but in the meantime your feedback on how well the new formula and factors work for you is encouraged.

The Isomerization Reaction and other Boil Losses

Since isomerization happens so slowly, and because it takes about 10 minutes for the alpha acids to get into solution so they can be isomerized, hop additions for 10 minutes or less have virtually no effect on the beer's bitterness. Yes, *some* iso-alphas will be formed in this short time, but when fermentation losses are accounted for, the percentage contributed by this is negligible. We can also assume that wort starting pH values are in the normal range for beer, around 5-5.5. We will also assume you have a vigorous boil. If you don't, you need to fix this problem as it will affect your beer in other ways besides poor utilization. The factors that remain are: boil time for each hop addition above 10 minutes, hopping rate (alpha acids vs. boil volume), boil gravity, boil temperature, the hop form (pellets or whole) and whether or not you use a hop bag.

The basic isomerization reaction proceeds rather slowly. As was mentioned earlier, there is some debate as to whether it peaks out at 2 hours or longer. In any case, a practical amount of time to boil your wort is no more than 90 minutes, so that's what we will assume in our calculations. The research into isomerization has shown that in water, the reaction proceeds at normal kinetic reaction rates. But in wort, the reaction slows down as the boil progresses. This is believed to be because the wort pH drops as the boil progresses, and isomerization is more efficient at higher pH values. Under ideal conditions, the maximum amount of isomerization after 90 minutes to 2 hours of boiling is around 70%.

The isomerization reaction is also affected by the hop rate. The more hops there are for a given volume of wort, the worse your final utilization will be. At a very minimal hop rate (around 40 mg/l of alpha acids introduced into the wort) isomerization is the most efficient. As the hopping rate rises, the reaction gets less and less efficient until we can't dissolve any more alpha acids in the wort.

What affects the hop rate? The main factor is the amount of hops you put in the boil and the amount of alpha acids in those hops. The hop rate is also dependent on the volume of the boil. The hop rate is really a measure of the alpha acids added to the boil for a given quantity of wort. For example, if we were boiling a wort of 20 liters (slightly over 5 gallons) and we added 50 grams (a little under 2 ounces) of hops to the wort that had 10% alpha acid, we would be adding a total of 5 grams or 5000 milligrams of alpha acids to the wort (10% of 50 grams = 5 grams, multiplied by 1000 to convert to milligrams = 5000 milligrams). To figure out how many mg/l of alpha acids we've added, just divide the milligrams by the number of liters, and in this case we get 250 mg/l of alpha acids in the wort. Now if we were doing a partial boil, and were only boiling 10 liters of wort (a little under 3 gallons), then our hopping rate would have doubled to 500 mg/l, and the hops will be utilized less efficiently.

For higher boil gravities (over 1.050) the gravity of the boil also seems to affect the isomerization reaction. Below 1.050 research has shown that boil gravity does not have any significant effect. But for partial boils the wort gravity will usually be above 1.050 so we need to account for the reduction in efficiency due to the higher gravity during the boil.

The temperature of the boil also has a effect on the isomerization reaction, and therefore on the utilization. Water boils at 212°F (100°C) at sea level. But what if you live in Denver? There water boils at around 201°F. That's actually a pretty significant difference. And it can make a big difference in your utilization. As an example, people have commented to me that homebrew guru Charlie Papazian's recipes all come out too bitter for their tastes. A possible explanation is that Charlie lives near Denver, and in order to get the right amount of bitterness in his brews he's had to adjust the hop rate upwards to account for his decreased utilization due to the lower boil temperature. When people make the identical recipe closer to sea level, now it calls for too large a quantity of hops.

As you should know by now, the alpha acids are contained in the hops' lupulin glands. In whole hops or plugs, almost all of these lupulin glands are intact. But in hop pellets, almost all of these glands have been burst. So when you add pellets to the boil, the alpha acids get into the wort a little quicker than with whole hops, so the isomerization reaction can start sooner. This time difference doesn't last long since the isomerization rate is so much slower than the extraction rate from whole hops. So eventually the whole hops isomerization rate will catch up to the pellets. What this means is that for hop additions with over 30 minutes of boil time, we don't need to correct for pellets vs. whole hops. But for additions between 10 and 30 minutes, we need to make an adjustment if we're using pellets.

Lastly, in order for the isomerization reaction to proceed efficiently, the hops need to be thrashing around in the boil. If you put your hops in a hop bag, the thrashing is greatly reduced. Hence you need to make an adjustment if you use a hop bag.

Whew! That's a lot of stuff going on in that wort. To summarize, alpha acids are being converted into iso-alpha acids, and under ideal conditions a maximum of 70% of the alpha acids put into the wort would be turned into isomerized alpha acids after 2 hours of boiling. But in the real world the number of iso-alpha acids that will be present after cooling the wort will be much smaller. The factors that affect this are the boil time, the boil gravity, the hopping rate, the temperature of the boil (based on the altitude of where we live), whether or not we're using pellets (for short boil times) and whether or not we use a hop bag. And that's just for the wort. Next we need to look into what happens during fermentation where more losses occur.

Fermentation Losses

If you have ever tasted unfermented wort, you know that not only does it taste sweet from the malt sugars, but it also tastes very bitter. Much more bitter than your final beer will be. That's because a significant amount of the bitterness is lost during fermentation. If we take into account the losses that happen during the boil, and subsequently those that happen during fermentation, then we will be able to do a better job of estimating the final bitterness of the beer.

Yeast plays a major role in the loss of iso-alpha acids. Some of the iso-alpha acids are actually adsorbed by the yeast (which means they stick to the yeast walls). The faster the yeast drops out of the beer (called flocculation), the less time there will be for the iso-alpha acids to attach themselves. Hence, more will be left in the beer and the beer will be more bitter. The converse is also true. Yeast that stays suspended for a long time will adsorb more iso-alpha acids and the beer will be less bitter, assuming the yeast finally drops out. If it stays suspended, or is purposely roused before drinking (as with a hefe-weizen - a beer meant to be cloudy with yeast), then you will taste all the bitterness. The amount of the yeast crop also has an effect. The more cells that grow, the more they can adsorb. But the amount of the yeast crop is not really under our control, so we'll only make adjustments for the yeast's flocculation characteristics. If finings are used to artificially change the flocculation characteristics, then that will also have to be taken into account.

The hop rate also plays a role in fermentation losses. As the hopping rate increases, so does the amount of iso-alpha acids that are lost. But at some point no more losses occur, most likely because the yeast cannot adsorb any more iso-alpha acids, and possibly also because the high alpha level has a inhibiting effect on the yeast growth. However, the point where this happens is well beyond the bitterness levels of normal beer, so we can basically ignore this effect, and this allows us to use a single hopping rate adjustment factor to account for boil and fermentation losses.

An important fermentation effect occurs as the yeast

releases CO_2 and creates a foam on the surface of the beer called the "dirty head". The dirty head is the first to form on the surface of the beer, usually followed by a yeast crop. This dirty head is where most of the iso-alpha acids are lost during fermentation. In effect, the CO_2 scrubs the iso-alpha acids out of the beer, and they tend to stay up there as the head continues to form. The iso-alpha acids start to oxidize up there and are bound up with other wort constituents and form a sticky mass that is no longer soluble in beer. If you are using the "blow-off" method of fermentation, then a lot of this material is blown out of the fermenter. Otherwise, it is pushed to the sides of the fermenter where it sticks. The little that does fall back through the beer won't redissolve. So in any case, these iso-alpha acids are lost. Now it turns out that the amount of iso-alpha acids lost in the dirty head is directly proportional to the wort's starting gravity. The higher the wort gravity, the higher the losses. This is another reason why worts of higher gravity have worse utilization (in addition to high boil gravities). The surface area of the fermenter also plays a role since some of the iso-alpha acids adhere to the fermenter walls. This explains why small batches sometimes don't scale up well to larger batches. The utilization of the large batch can be better because the larger containers usually have a smaller surface area-to-volume ratio than smaller containers.

Lastly, if you filter the beer you will lose some iso-alphas in this process. You will also get some losses if you pasteurize the beer, but not many home or microbrewers will be doing this.

Since the hopping rate and gravity effects that happen during the boil are generally proportional to those that happen during fermentation, we don't need separate boil and fermentation correction factors for each. This allows us to use a single correction factor for each to correct for both the boil and fermentation effects. Therefore, what remains are the yeast and filtration effects, and these will have their own factors.

The IBU Prediction Formula

The formula that follows is based primarily on the formula published by Jackie Rager in the 1990 *Zymurgy* special issue on hops. This formula (with corrections and modifications) has been used successfully by thousands of brewers (including me). Rather than rework the basic structure of the formula to include all these new factors, I have chosen to keep its structure pretty much the same and therefore familiar. The numbers we plug into the formula are what have been improved, and more brewing variables can be accounted for at your option. Rager's original formula looked like this (for English units):

$$\text{hop wt. in ozs} = \frac{\text{Volume in Gallons} * (1+GA) * \text{IBUs Desired}}{\% \text{ Util} * \% \text{ Alpha} * 7490}$$

The revised formula looks identical except CA (combined adjustments) has replaced 1+GA (the gravity adjustment):

$$\text{hop wt. in ozs} = \frac{\text{Volume in Gallons} * CA * \text{IBUs Desired}}{\% \text{ Util} * \% \text{ Alpha} * 0.749}$$

In Rager's original article he published a table of utilization based on boil time. The times ranged from 0-60 minutes and the values he used were pretty optimistic. I have reworked the table with new utilization values and extended the time to 90 minutes. The new values are a better representation of the actual curve of utilization vs. boil time and are also more realistic. For reference I have included Rager's original numbers in the table as well.

The only correction factor Rager allowed for was boil gravity. For a certain range of beers (not too bitter and not too high in gravity) this single factor seems to work well.

But for beers outside this range, more correction needs to be done. I have added correction factors for the hopping rate, boil temperature, the yeast characteristics, filtration, whether or not you are using pellets and/or a hop bag during the boil. You can choose to either use these new factors or ignore them at your option.

Before we begin, you need to decide how many bittering hop additions you would like to make. Many brewers (on all scales) make only one bittering addition at or near the start of the boil. Some also make intermediate additions at some point in the boil, usually about 30 minutes or so before knockout (which means the end of the boil). The idea is to provide a hint of hoppy character to the beer without wasting the alpha acids entirely (which is the case for standard late-hop aroma additions). While this might make some sense for large operations where those few pennies saved in alpha acids add up, for us smaller brewers I can't see the point. The aroma imparted from this addition will be negligible, and if you add any hops for aroma later, you'll never tell the difference. The utilization from this addition will be quite poor, especially if you use whole hops. In my opinion, you would be better off adding more hops at the beginning of the boil and then hops for aroma at the end, and don't bother with any intermediate additions. It also makes the calculations easier.

Step-by-step Predictions of Utilization and IBUs

What follows are the step-by-step instructions for predicting how many ounces of hops to add to get a certain number of IBUs (for those that want to work in metric units, use the alternate formula at the end of this section).

First we will calculate our correction factors and then combine them into a single correction factor. Then we'll look up our base utilization percentage and perform the calculation which will tell us how many ounces of hops to use to reach our target bitterness level.

Step 1. Calculate the wort concentration factor (CF). If you are using a partial boil, we need to calculate your "concentration factor" (CF) which we will use to adjust the boil gravity and hopping rate factors. Use the formula:

CF = Final Volume / Boil Volume

For example, you boil three gallons of wort but add two gallons of water prior to pitching to get a final batch volume of five gallons, then 5 / 3 = 1.7 (rounded up). If you do full boils, CF=1. Also note that the units you use (gallons, liters or barrels) doesn't matter.

Step 2. Calculate the Boil Gravity (BG). If you are using a full boil, then your boil gravity is equal to the starting gravity. You can skip this step if you'd like, or the formula still works if CF=1. Calculate your boil gravity (BG) using the formula:

BG = (CF * (Starting Gravity -1)) + 1

If our wort starting gravity is 1.045 but we're doing a partial boil as in step 1 then BG = (1.7 * (1.045 -1) + 1 which equals 1.076 (rounded).

Step 3. Calculate the Gravity Factor (GF). If the value you calculated for BG in step 2 is less than 1.050 then the Gravity Factor (GF) is 1. If BG is greater than 1.050 then calculate GF using the following formula:

GF = ((BG - 1.050) / .2) +1

Using our partial boil example above, ((1.076 - 1.050) / .2) + 1 = 1.13. Note that this value is the same as Rager's (GA+1) value, and can be substituted directly.

Step 4. Calculate the Hopping Rate Factor (HF). Use the formula:

HF = ((CF * Desired IBUs) / 260) + 1

where CF is what we calculated in step 2 and Desired IBUs is the number of IBUs we want in our beer from this hop addition. If we wanted 35 IBUs from this hop addition, and using our partial boil example above, the formula looks like ((1.7 * 35) / 260)+ 1 which equals 1.23 (rounded).

Step 5. Calculate the Temperature Factor (TF). To do this step you need to know the elevation in feet where you live (or where you are brewing). You can find this out by calling your city hall, chamber of commerce or driving around looking for those "City Limits" signs that usually list the population and the elevation (like the one I'm standing next to on the back cover of this book). If you live pretty close to sea level then TF = 1. Otherwise use the formula:

TF = ((Elevation in Feet / 550) * 0.02) + 1

If we lived at 1100 feet above sea level, then the formula would look like ((1100 / 550) * 0.02) + 1 which is 1.04. Note that if you live below sea level, then use a negative number for the elevation.

Step 6. Combine all the above factors to create a Combined Adjustment factor (CA). Do this by multiplying them all together:

CA = GF * HF * TF

Following along with our example, GF was 1.13, HF was 1.23 and TF was 1.04, and 1.13 * 1.23 * 1.04 = 1.45 (rounded).

Using Hops

Boil Time	Rager	% Util
< 6 min.	5%	0%
6-10 min.	6%	0%
11-15 min.	8%	2%
16-20 min.	10.10%	5%
21-25 min.	12.10%	8%
26-30 min.	15.30%	11%
31-35 min.	18.80%	14%
36-40 min.	22.80%	16%
41-45 min.	26.90%	18%
46-50 min.	28.10%	19%
51-60 min.	30%	20%
61-70 min.	-	21%
71-80 min.	-	22%
81-90 min.	-	23%

Table 8-1   Use to find % Util based on your boil time. Note that the "Rager" column is provided mainly as a reference. Use of the "% Util" column is recommended.

Step 7. Calculate the number of ounces of hops we need. To do this you will need to know the alpha acid percentage of the hops you are using. You will need to look up the base utilization percentage from table 8-1, based on the amount of boil time. (Use the "% Util" column, Rager's numbers are mainly provided for reference.) Now use the formula:

$$\text{hop wt. in ozs} = \frac{\text{Volume in Gallons * CA * IBUs Desired}}{\text{\% Util * \% Alpha * 0.749}}$$

Note that Rager's original formula had you use the decimal equivalents of the % Util and the % Alpha which meant that 21% would be expressed as 0.21, but I have changed the 7490 constant to 0.749 so you can now use the whole percentage numbers (21% = 21). In our example, the top half of the equation looks like 5 * 1.45 * 35 which is 253.75. If the hops we are using had 6% alpha acids and we are boiling for 60 minutes, then the bottom half of the equation looks like 20 * 6 * 0.749 which equals 89.88 and then we divide 253.75 by 89.88 to get 2.82 ounces of hops. In actual practice, you would round this number to something more convenient to measure, like 2 3/4 ounces (2.75).

If you want to use metric units (liters of wort and grams of hops instead of gallons and ounces) use the following formula instead:

$$\text{hop wt. in gms} \quad \frac{\text{Volume in Liters * CA * IBUs Desired}}{\text{\% Util * \% Alpha * 0.1}}$$

Getting Simpler

The procedure presented above may seem a lot more complex than Rager's original formula, but really all we have added are the factors for the hop rate and the boil temperature. The three adjustment factors above (gravity, hop rate and boil temperature) are the three I consider essential to getting more accurate results than the original formula (in addition to the revised utilization table). But you are free to leave any or all of them out if you wish.

If you live near sea level, you can omit the Temperature Factor (TF) calculation. Likewise if you always do full volume boils you can eliminate the Concentration Factor (CF) calculation and therefore eliminate the GB calculation and simplify the HF calculation. GB simply becomes the wort starting gravity and HF simply becomes

(IBUs / 260) + 1. If you are doing a full boil and the wort gravity is less than 1.050, then you can eliminate the GB and GF calculations altogether.

Getting More Complicated

Above I stated that I felt the three adjustment factors (boil gravity, hop rate and boil temperature) were the minimum required for a good IBU estimation. But there are also considerations we can optionally account for, depending on how complex you want to get (and theoretically more accurate). We can also adjust for the yeast characteristics, pellets vs. whole hops, whether or not we use a hop bag and filtration if applicable.

You can either continue to build on the Combined Adjustment Factor (CA) or just adjust the final result of the main calculation. I'll show you how to do it both ways.

To adjust for yeast characteristics, you need to know the flocculation characteristics of your yeast. Most yeast is "normal" but some yeast can take a long time to drop out and others clear quickly. The depth of the fermenter can also play a role: shallow fermenters allow the yeast to drop more quickly because it has less distance to fall. Finings can turn a slow flocculating yeast into a fast one. You should ask your yeast supplier what flocculation characteristics your yeast has, but don't forget to think about how you or the fermenter geometry might affect things. If you can't find any data on your yeast, it's usually a safe bet that it's normal, so you can skip any yeast adjustment. If your yeast is a fast flocculator, then your utilization will be increased by about 5%, so you want to decrease the amount of hops by 5% to compensate. You can do this directly with the hop amount (multiply it by 0.95). Similarly, if the yeast is a slow flocculator, then your utilization will be decreased by about 5% so you need to increase the amount of hops by 5% to compensate (multiply by 1.05). If the beer is a hefe-weizen, then all of the bitterness normally adsorbed by the yeast (and lost) will still be in the beer. You will taste it when you drink the beer, hence your effective utilization is higher. Compensate by decreasing the amount of hops by 20% (multiply by 0.80).

If you are using pellets and the boil time of the addition you are calculating is greater than 10 minutes but less than 30 minutes, then your utilization will be increased by about 10%. To compensate for this, decrease the amount of hops by 10% (multiply by 0.9). Of course if you are using whole hops or plugs, or your boil time is greater than 30 minutes, you don't need to worry about it.

If you use a hop bag to boil your hops in, then your utilization will be decreased by about 10%, assuming you haven't stuffed the bag full, making it hard for the wort to get at the hops. If it is, consider using two bags or your utilization will be decreased even further. For a loosely filled hop bag, compensate by increasing the amount of hops by 10% (multiply by 1.10). For a stuffed full hop bag, multiply by 1.20 or more.

Lastly, if you filter the beer your utilization will be decreased by 1.25% to 2.5% depending on how aggressive your filtration is. You should increase the amount of hops to compensate by multiplying the amount by 1.0125 to 1.025 (you'll have to derive the exact figure that works for you experimentally).

You can also build the above adjustment factors into the Combined Adjustment (CA) formula. If we called the yeast factor YF, the pellet factor PF, the bag factor BF and the Filter Factor FF, then the complete CA formula would look like:

$$CA = GF * HF * TF * YF * PF * BF * FF$$

Again, feel free to leave out any of these factors that don't apply to you or you feel are unnecessary.

:ulating Your Final Utilization

If you want to know your final utilization, then we first need to convert the amount of hops we put in the wort to milligrams per liter of alpha acid. If you work in grams of hops and liters of wort, this is pretty straightforward. Multiply the grams of hops by the alpha acid percentage (as a decimal equivalent) to get the grams of alpha acid added to the wort and then multiply that value by 1000 to convert to milligrams. Now divide this number by the number of liters in your final batch size to get the milligrams/liter. If you used gallons and ounces, then use the formula (where Alpha % is now a whole number):

(Alpha % * Hop Wt. in Ozs * 74.9) / Gallons

to get milligrams per liter of alpha acids added to the wort.

To calculate the utilization, divide the IBUs by the mg/l of alpha acids you just calculated and multiply the result by 100. That will give you the percentage utilization. In the example we've been using throughout, our batch size was 5 gallons, we determined we needed 2.82 ounces of 6% alpha hops to give us 35 IBUs. So first we convert the hop addition to mg/l of alpha acids: (6 * 2.82 * 74.9) / 5 = 253 mg/l (rounded) of alpha acids added to the wort. Dividing 35 by 253 and then multiplying by 100 gives us 13.8% utilization (if that sounds low, don't forget that in our example we used a partial boil for only 60 minutes, a good amount of bitterness and starting gravity, and brewed at 1100 feet).

Working the IBU Formula Backwards

Sometimes it's useful to be able to work the IBU calculation backwards, meaning you'd like to know how many IBUs you'll get from a given weight of hops. This is useful if you have only a certain amount of hops on hand you want to know if there's enough to reach your target bitterness or not. It's also useful to figure out how many IBUs a recipe will give you if all the recipe contains is the hop weight and alphas or AAUs/HBUs.

Unfortunately there is a slight problem. Remember that we figured our hop rate correction factor (HF) based on the number of IBUs we wanted. Now we are trying to *solve* for IBUs and since we don't yet know what that number is, we can't do a hop rate factor calculation. There *is* a mathematical solution to the problem, but it's very complicated. The simplest thing to do is to take a guess at the number of IBUs and perform the IBU calculation to see how close you come to the hop weight you wanted to solve for. The following equations can be used to get you in the ballpark, but the result will always be too high since the CA equation would be missing HF. So adjust the result of the equation downward and plug that number into the IBU calculation and see how close you are to the weight you are solving for (don't forget to calculate HF based on your trial value). Chances are you'll be a bit off, so change the IBU value (and HF) accordingly and try again. You'll have to keep this up until your result equals the hop weight.

$$\text{Approx. IBUs} = \frac{\text{Hop Wt. in Ozs * \% Util * \% Alpha * 0.749}}{\text{Volume in Gallons * CA}}$$

$$\text{Approx. IBUs} = \frac{\text{Hop Wt. in gms * \% Util * \% Alpha * 0.1}}{\text{Volume in Liters * CA}}$$

Here's an example: Let's say we have 1.5 ounces of hops that have 7% alpha acid and we want to know how many IBUs that will give us in our beer. We are making 5 gallons with an SG of 1.045, we're doing a full boil for 90 minutes and we live near sea level. Because our SG is below

143

Using Hops

1.050 and we live at sea level, the only factor in CA we care about is the hopping rate factor (HF), but for the first equation we leave it out too. Using the formula for ounces above: 1.5 * 23 * 7 * 0.749 = 180.88 and we divide that by 5 (since we have no factors yet for CA) to get about 36 IBUs. We know this number is too high, so lets reduce it to 32 IBUs. Now we figure the HF value using 32 IBUs. Since we're doing a full boil, HF = (IBUs / 260) +1 which is 1.12 (rounded). Now we do the IBU calculation: 5 * 1.12 * 32 = 179 (rounded) and 23 * 7 * 0.749 = 121 (rounded). 180 / 121 = 1.49 ounces and that's more than close enough. So now we know that our addition of 1.5 ounces of 7% alpha hops will give us 32 IBUs.

Converting AAUs/HBUs to IBUs

If you have a recipe in HBUs or AAUs and you want to know how many IBUs it will have, then you can convert HBUs/AAUs into IBUs. AAUs/HBUs are just the amount of alpha acids in 1 ounce of hops, and the total number of AAUs/HBUs is calculated by multiplying the hop weight times the alpha acid percentage. If you look at the "English units" equation in the previous section that solves for IBUs, you can see that both the hop weight and alpha acid percentage are multiplied on the top line. Therefore we can use the same procedure above and only modify the formula slightly for HBUs/AAUs. The modified formula looks like:

$$\text{Approx. IBUs} = \frac{\text{AAUs * \% Util * 0.749}}{\text{Volume in Gallons * CA}}$$

Be sure to use the procedure in the previous section to adjust for hopping rate and get the IBU value closer.

144

Correlating Actual vs. Predicted Utilization

Even though I have tried to provide you with a good method of predicting your utilization (and taking your choice of the major brewing variables into account), there are still many other variables that can come into play. Therefore, while the methods I've presented will get you very close in most cases, there may still be factors in your own brewing process that will affect the results. It would be nice to be able to correlate the predicted results with your actual results. You can then make adjustments to the formula to zero in on your actual utilization.

The best way to do this is with actual laboratory measurements of your beer's bitterness. As was mentioned earlier, the cost of the equipment to do this is beyond the reach of homebrewers and most microbrewers. There are several labs that will measure your beer's bitterness for a fee. Until recently, they catered mainly to the professional brewer. But now some services oriented towards the homebrewer have started to appear. If you are willing to spend the $25-50 to have your beer analyzed, this is the best way to go.

In the future, I am confident that you will see some "Home IBU Test Kits" on the market. Until then, here is a method by which you can test your beer's bitterness within a few IBUs of accuracy:

The Taste-Titration Method of Estimating IBUs

The taste-titration method of estimating IBUs uses one of the most sensitive sensor-arrays known: your taste buds! In short, the method consists of taking a beer of known bitterness, adding iso-alpha extract to the beer an IBU or so at a time, and tasting against the beer you want to know the IBU rating of. When the two beers taste equally bitter, you add the amount of IBUs that were present in the base beer to the amount you added to make the beers taste equally bitter, and the result should be close to the IBUs of the beer you were testing. To use this method, you will need some calibrated iso-alpha extract, an eye dropper, a 1/8th tsp measure, a small glass (like a shot glass), two beer glasses and a beer of known IBUs that is similar in style to the beer you want to know the IBUs of.

Calibrated iso-alpha extract is available from the author's company HopTech, and potentially from other sources. Since I am most familiar with the HopTech product, the examples given here will assume that product's calibration (1/8 tsp = 1 IBU in 5 gallons). If you use a product with a different calibration, you will need to figure out how to adjust this procedure accordingly for that product's strength.

An eye dropper can be obtained at your local pharmacy, and the 1/8th tsp measure is probably already in your kitchen. You'll need two beer glasses that can hold at least 6 ounces of beer with a few ounces of headroom. The glasses should be identical. Make a mark on one of them at 6 ounces with a piece of tape. You'll also need a small glass (a shot glass is ideal) for diluting the extract.

The hardest part is finding a beer of known IBUs that is similar in style to the beer you want to test. This beer should also be lower (or equal) in IBUs to the beer you want to test. I suggest you get a copy of Fred Eckhardt's book *The Essentials of Beer Style*. This book lists a large number of commercially available beers and their IBU ratings. The book is stocked by homebrew suppliers and is also available directly from the author at Fred Eckhardt Communications, P.O. Box 546, Portland, Oregon, 97207. I suggest you write for current pricing and shipping costs. Be aware that breweries change their beer's IBU ratings all the time, so Fred's book should be taken as a general guide, not gospel. Once you find a beer that fits, you can call the brewery and ask if they'll tell you the current IBU rating. If all else fails, you can always use Budweiser. Because it's not similar to any beer you're likely to brew, your results won't be quite as accurate, but it will probably be close enough. The following examples assume the use of Bud (currently about 11 IBUs).

Step 1: Since all eye-droppers make different size drops, we need to determine how big a drop your eye-dropper makes. We do this by filling the eye-dropper with water and filling the 1/8 tsp measure to the top, counting the number of drops it takes. Do this a few times. If you always get the same result, great. If not, take the average result. If you keep this eye dropper, you only need to do this step once, as long as you remember the number of drops.

Step 2: Since the Iso-Alpha Extract is so strong (for use in 6 ozs of beer), we need to dilute it before we can use it. Take the shot glass or other small container and add 1/2 oz of water to it. Ideally you should use distilled water, but it's not really necessary if your tap water is decent. (One tablespoon equals 1/2 oz, by the way). To this add 1/4 tsp of the HopTech Iso-Alpha Extract and stir well.

Step 3: Put about 6 ozs of the beer you want to test (called Beer A from now on) into the beer glass without the 6 oz mark. The exact amount of Beer A doesn't matter. Put exactly 6 ozs of Bud (from now on called Beer B) in the glass with the mark on it.

Your eye dropper has this many drops in 1/8th tsp.	Iso-Alpha Extract Diluted 1/4 tsp in 1/2 oz water IBU/Drop in 6 ozs
10	0.88
11	0.80
12	0.74
13	0.68
14	0.64
15	0.60
16	0.56
17	0.52
18	0.50
19	0.46
20	0.44
21	0.42
22	0.40
23	0.38
24	0.37
25	0.36

Table 8-2. Eye-dropper calibration table.

Step 4: If you have a rough idea of Beer A's bitterness, subtract about 5 IBUs from it and then using table 8-2, adjust Beer B's bitterness to this IBU rating by adding drops of the diluted iso-alpha extract to Beer B and stirring it gently, but thoroughly. For example, let's say you think Beer A has 30 IBUs. Subtracting 5 from that gives us 25 IBUs. Beer B (Bud) has 11 IBUs, so we need to add 14 IBUs to Beer B to get it to 25 IBUs. If our eye-dropper had 20 drops per 1/8 tsp, then according to table 8-2 each drop equals 0.44 IBUs. Dividing 14 by 0.44 gives us about 32 drops. So we add 32 drops of the diluted extract to Beer B. Beer B will now be a 25 IBU Bud (it's amazing how much better it gets).

Step 5: Taste the two beers and determine if Beer A's bitterness equals Beer B's.

Step 6: If Beer A's bitterness is less than Beer B's, then add a drop (or two) to Beer B and stir gently and taste again. Repeat Steps 5 and 6 until Beer B's bitterness is the same as Beer A. Make sure you keep track of how many drops you add. If Beer B's volume gets down a couple of ounces, you should discard it and refill the glass with a fresh 6 ozs of Beer B and then add the number of drops of extract you added in Step 4 plus all the drops you have added up till now. The reason for this is that as you drink Beer B its volume gets lower, and the IBUs/drop calibration gets progressively stronger, and therefore the error gets bigger.

Step 7: Once the two beers have equal bitterness, add up the total number of drops it took to get there and multiply by the IBU/drop. Now add the IBU rating of Beer B and this will give you the IBU rating of your beer. For example, if our eye-dropper gives 0.44 IBUs per drop and we added 50 drops (total), 50 * 0.44 = 22. Beer B had 11 IBUs to start with, so 22+11= 33 IBUs. So your beer is equal to approximately 33 IBUs.

Step 8: Once you think you have zeroed in on the IBUs, repeat the test one more time, but this time add the right amount of drops to Beer B to equal the exact bitterness that you determined Beer A was. If they are still equal, you are done. If they aren't, it means that changing Beer B's volume while drinking it has had too much of an effect, so try again until you get it right.

As I mentioned before, your results will be more accurate if you can find a beer that is close in style to the beer you are measuring. If you use Bud, the error will get worse the darker and more full bodied your beer is. It also helps to have a friend or two taste the beers with you. If you all agree, then you have no doubts. If you all disagree wildly (more than 3-5 IBUs), something is wrong or you need to find new friends! In a real professional taste test, "triangle" tasting would be used. This is where three beers are used: two of the beers are identical and the third is different. The idea is to make sure that the tasters can consistently identify the two identical beers as being the same. If the taster can't, then the results are not valid. This works well if the two beers are extremely close in style and the taster is trying to sense subtle differences. In our case, the two beers are likely to be far enough different that it would be easy to pick out the two identical beers.

What if you find a beer that is close in style but *higher* in IBUs than you think your beer is? All you need to do is use your beer for Beer B and the commercial beer as Beer A. Now you'll be adjusting your beer's bitterness upwards until it matches Beer A. Subtract (rather than add) the number of IBUs you added from the number in the commercial beer and you will have the IBUs in your beer.

The accuracy of this technique depends on a lot of factors, not the least of which is how close the two beer styles are, but also how good a taster you are. The common wisdom is that experienced tasters can sense about a 2-3 IBU difference reliably, so that is about as accurate as you can expect to get with this method. But the more you practice, the more accurate you will get.

A good way to practice this technique is by having a friend make Beer A from Bud by adding drops of the diluted extract to a certain IBU rating. Then make up Beer B to some number of IBUs less than Beer A, also using Bud. The friend shouldn't tell you anything, but let you start testing Beer B and see how close you get. Since you are using the same base beer, you should be able to get very accurate results. You can now also use the triangle tasting method since all the beers are so similar.

This is also a great activity for a homebrew club meeting. If you do this as a group, you will need to prepare separate glass sets for every couple of people to keep Beer B's volume at a reasonable level for a few rounds. Alternatively you can refill Beer B and add new drops for each round. You can also use smaller amounts of Beer B by adjusting the IBU/drop accordingly. For example, for 3 ounces of Beer B, the IBUs drop would be doubled since the volume is now halved. Lastly, an interesting test of your taste buds is to have someone prepare glasses of beer at varying IBU ratings and then arrange them in random order. Now have the group guess the actual IBU rating of the beers to see how close they can come.

Chapter 9 - Using Hops for Bittering

In the previous chapter, we discussed everything you ever wanted to know (and then some) about how and why hops bitter the beer, and how to predict how bitter your beer will be and the quantity of hops to add. In this chapter we're going to talk about how to actually use the hops and hop products to bitter your beer.

When to Add Bittering Hops

If you got through the previous chapter, you now understand that the longer you boil your hops (up to two hours), the more bitterness you will get out of them. But the reaction is not linear. You will get much more out of increasing the boiling time from 30 to 60 minutes than you will from 60 to 90 minutes. Similarly, you will get more out of increasing the boiling time from 60 to 90 minutes than you will from 90 to 120 minutes. You will get the most out of them at 120 minutes, but the difference between 90 and 120 is very small. If you factor in your time and energy costs, the optimum boil time is somewhere between 60 and 90 minutes. Personally, I like to boil my wort and hops for 90 minutes. For my all-grain brewing setup, this gives me about the right amount of volume reduction in the boil.

When I was an extract brewer and doing partial boils, I preferred 60 minutes.

There are many schools of thought on exactly when to add the hops. The most common method is to add them right at the beginning of the boil. Some brewers believe that waiting until you see the first signs of the "hot break" is the right time. The theory is that when the hot break forms, it will bind up some of the hop resins present, and thus your utilization will suffer. The arguments against this are that in order to get a good hot break, you need the hops to be there. Also any better utilization that might be obtained due to the lack of binding would be offset by the longer boil time if the hops were just added at the beginning of the boil. It also seems that it is mostly the hop tannins (not the resins or alpha acids) that are bound up by the hot break. Lastly, the presence of the hops lowers the surface tension of the wort, helping to prevent boil-overs, and boil-overs are more likely in the first few minutes of the boil. So what's the answer? You can make good beer both ways, there's no doubt. I prefer to add them at the beginning. It's clear to me that this makes the most sense. But it's a "religious" issue and there is no convincing some brewers. You can add them after the boil has been going about 10 minutes if you like. Just remember to start timing when you add the hops, not when the boil starts.

In the previous chapter, we discussed multiple bittering additions. Some brewers add all of the bittering hops at (or near) the beginning of the boil. Some add only a portion of the bittering hops at the beginning, and then add some more about half-way through or about 30 minutes before the end of the boil. The theory is that this second addition of hops will serve a dual purpose of adding some bittering and some hop character. In a very light beer that has no finishing hops (those added near the end of the boil), this might work. But I can't really see the point. The hop character contributed by these hops will be very slight and the bittering will be very inefficient. I'm a believer in adding all your bittering hops at the beginning, and if you want hop character and aroma, then add the hops near the end of the boil. It also makes the bittering calculations much easier and more precise.

How Bitter Should My Beer Be?

The "correct" bitterness of your beer is largely a matter of personal taste. Traditionally, certain beers are expected to have a certain range of bitterness associated with that style. At a minimum, the beer's bitterness should be balanced with the other flavors, and a lot of this depends on the beer's style. The only time you should really be concerned about being "true-to-style" is if you're entering a contest. And even then the American Homebrewer's Association gives you pretty wide latitude of bitterness for most styles. Still, if you make an IPA and it only has 20 IBUs, (40-60 is the norm) and you *call* it an IPA, people who "know what an IPA is supposed to be" will think something is wrong with your beer. Given this, you'd probably still like to know what the typical IBU range is for traditional beer styles. The following is a table of beer styles with their typical IBUs, based on the AHA style guidelines:

Style	IBUs
Barley Wine	50-100
Belgian Brown Ale	15-25
Belgian White (Wit)	15-25
Belgian Trappist House and Doubles	10-25
Belgian Trappist Triples	14-25
Saison	20-30
Lambics	11-23
English Mild	14-20
English Brown Ale	15-25
American Brown Ale	25-60

English Pale Ale	20-40
India Pale Ale (IPA)	40-60
American Pale Ale	20-40
English Ordinary Bitter	20-25
English Extra Special Bitter (ESB)	30-35
Scottish Light Ale	10-15
Scottish Heavy	12-17
Scottish Export	15-20
Robust Porter	25-40
Brown Porter	20-30
English Old/Strong Ale	30-40
Scotch Strong Ale	25-35
Dry Stout	30-40
Sweet (Cream) Stout	15-25
Imperial Stout	50-80
German Bock	20-30
Helles (Pale) Bock	20-35
Dopplebock	17-27
Dunkel	16-25
American Dark Lager	14-20
Dortmund/Export	23-29
Munich Helles	18-25
Classic Pilsner	35-45
German Pilsner	30-40
American "Lite" Lager	8-17
American Lager	5-15
American Premium Lager	13-23
American "Dry" Lager	15-23
American Wheat Beer	5-17
Vienna	22-28
Marzen/Octoberfest	22-28
Alt Beer	25-35
Kolsch	20-30
Cream Ale	10-22
Fruit Ale	Varies a lot
Herbed and Spiced Beer	Varies a lot
Smoked Beer	20-30
Anchor Steam Style *	33-45
Berliner Weisse	3-6
German Weizen and Hefe-weizen	10-15

* Steam Beer is a trademark of Anchor Brewing and may not be used by any brewery for commercial purposes. It is also known as California Common Beer.

For more information on styles and their bittering, I recommend the *Zymurgy* 1991 Special Issue on *Classic Beer Styles* and Fred Eckhardt's book *The Essentials of Beer Style*.

Also, don't be afraid to go "out-of-style". How else will we ever get new styles?

What Kind of Hops Should I Use?

Chapter 4 lists all of the commonly available hops, and separates them into bittering and aroma hop categories. It also lists some of the beer styles that are appropriate for each type of hop, but this is mainly for a hop's aroma, not for bittering. Even so, each hop has its own unique "signature" when it comes to bittering. Some have a harsher bitter flavor than others, and some are especially smooth and clean in their bitter character. These kind of distinctions are also listed with the hop variety. Some are quite recognizable. For example, nine times out of ten I can pick out a beer that has been bittered with Chinook. Mainly because I don't happen to like the bitter character of Chinook. But, most brewers don't agree with me. Basically, you'll forgive the pun, it all boils down to what you like in your beer. I urge you to experiment with different hop varieties to see what you like. What is one brewers "poison" is another brewer's "passion". If you're in doubt as to which hop to use for bittering, you can't go wrong with any of the hops listed as being neutral in character, or going with the main *aroma* hop as a bittering hop as well.

Hops For Lambics

Usually we want the freshest hops we can get. But there is one style of beer that calls for the oldest hops you can get, and that's Lambics. Lambics have almost no hop bitterness, but brewers desired the preservative qualities of the hop. So they let the hops age at room temperature for about 3 years until they have turned quite brown and any objectionable aromas and flavors due to oxidation are gone. Amazingly, the hops still have a preservative effect, but they will impart no bitterness, character or aroma to the beer.

You can also let some hops age for three years, but three years planning ahead doesn't fit the brewing schedules of most of the brewers I know. We're lucky if we get the yeast started on time! But there are a couple of options: The first is just to ignore the need for the old hops. If the beer will all be consumed in a short amount of time (and you are making a pseudo-lambic that won't be aged for a long time) then the extra preservative qualities probably aren't that necessary. The other option is to artificially age the hops. You can do this by putting them in a thin layer on a tray in a warm oven (no more than 150°F) for anywhere between 12 and 48 hours. They are done when they have all turned brown, have no trace of aroma and don't taste bitter when you chew on them. It really doesn't matter what kind of hops you use, but they should be whole hops and the lowest alpha you can find. This is a good use for "closeout" hops from last year's crop.

Some warnings are in order if you want to age your own hops: They are going to stink for while. Make sure anyone else you may live with is prepared for this. You don't want to ruin a relationship just for a lambic (I hope). Make sure the oven doesn't get too warm, you don't want to risk setting the hops on fire.

What About Aroma Hops For Bittering?

One school of thought says "Alpha is alpha is alpha!"

In other words, it doesn't matter what you use for bittering, as long as you boil for an adequate amount of time (uncovered), so you might as well use high-alpha hops for bittering and save your aroma hops for late additions and for dry hopping. This might be true for some beers, as long as you use a neutral bittering hop that has no identifiable signature. But some beers, especially pilsners and lighter lagers, really want the aroma hop used in the finish to also be used for bittering. This is especially true if there is a light amount or no finishing hops. Why? While it is true that *most* of the hop oils and flavor components are lost during the boil, *some* survive. And if the beer is especially clean, the taste will come through. Lastly, aroma hops tend to have very low levels of cohumulone (one of the alpha acids). High levels of cohumulone are thought to give the beer a harsher bitterness. You can also choose a high alpha hop with relatively low levels of cohumulone, but an aroma hop is usually a sure bet. Like most things in brewing, there are no hard answers, but there are also no rules. This is where the "art" of brewing comes into play. Again, I urge you to experiment.

Other Factors That Affect a Beer's Perceived Bitterness

While hops are the primary ingredient in beer that affect the beer's bitterness, several other of the beer's ingredients can also either mask or enhance a beer's bitterness.

The more "malty" character a beer has, the more it can mask the beer's bitterness. This is usually OK, because malty beers are meant to be just that, and the bitterness should take a back seat. Still, the bitterness should be nicely balanced with the malt, and this may require a bit more bitterness than if the beer was less malty.

Similarly, a flavorful, heavy beer can mask quite bit of the bitterness. Again this may require a bit more bitterness to compensate or balance with the other flavors.

Dark specialty grains, especially the highly roasted malts like black patent, can add a significant bitter character of their own. If your beer (typically only a stout or porter) has a high proportion of these grains, you would do well to back off on the hops a bit. The bitterness from these grains can be quite astringent and unpleasant, though. So I would recommend you back off on the dark grains and increase the hops. But that's just my opinion.

If your brewing water has a high carbonate content (either naturally or added by you), this will tend to "mellow" the beer's bitterness. On the other hand, if your water has a lot of sulfate in it, then this can have the opposite effect, giving the beer a dry, harsh edge. This can be balanced by carbonate, however. High amounts of magnesium can have its own bitterness (and also act as a laxative).

Lastly, hop oils from liberal amounts of finish or dry hopping will increase the perception of the beer's bitterness. Usually this is fine, as it goes with the style of beer that begs for lots of hop character and aroma.

Whole Hops vs. Pellets in the Brew Kettle

We've talked about this subject in some depth in previous chapters, but here is a quick summary: For boil times of greater than 10 minutes and less than 30 minutes, pellets will be more efficient than whole hops. But for longer boil times, it really doesn't matter. (Shorter times are for hop character and aroma, dealt with in the next two chapters). Separating the wort from the hops is the biggest issue. Briefly, whole hops are easily strained from the wort, and pellet particles are not. See Chapter 5's section on *Whole vs. Pellets* for tips on how to deal with both of them.

Avoiding Boil-Overs

You may have discovered that if you have nice rolling boil going and you toss in some hops, the kettle starts to look like Mt. Vesuvius. "But didn't you just say that hops *prevented* boil-overs? Now you're telling me it causes them?" Both are true. Once the hops are in the wort, they help to prevent boil overs. But right when you add them, they can cause a big one!

The reason is that the bubbles we associate with boiling occur because the water vaporizes into steam and creates steam bubbles that rise to the surface. The bubble can start to form anywhere, but it has the easiest time forming at a rough spot in the kettle. This is known as a nucleation point. When you add the hops to a vigorously boiling wort, you're instantly adding thousands of nucleation points. Thousands of extra bubbles are formed and that causes the boil-over.

This is more prone to happen when adding pellets, but it can happen with whole hops too. There is a very easy way to keep it from happening: turn down the heat right before you add the hops. Stir the hops in and turn the heat back up. It seems so simple, but a lot of brewers haven't thought to do it. If you have an electric stove, wait a few minutes for the wort to stop boiling. You can also add the hops slowly, but I like the first method. A boil-over is more likely to occur with the first hop addition, but it can happen with the late additions as well.

Using a Hop Bag

Some brewers prefer to avoid the mess of straining all of the hop pieces out of the wort by putting their hops in a mesh bag during boiling. One simply pulls the bag out of the wort at the end of the boil to get rid of the hops. There are many different hop bags on the market. Some have wide mesh and others have fine mesh. Some are made of nylon and some are made of cotton or muslin. They all work, but they can work differently.

Bags with a wide mesh and even the fine mesh nylon bags are really only suitable for whole hops. They won't keep pellet particles contained. There are some fine mesh cotton bags on the market that will contain pellet particles during the boil, and also work for whole hops.

One is advised not to stuff the bags full as this will inhibit the wort from getting at the hops and will cause a loss of efficiency. You will already get about a 10% loss just by using a loosely filled bag, and stuffing it full makes the losses worse. When using one of the fine mesh cotton bags with pellets, one is especially cautioned on this point. The bags look like they can hold quite a large amount of pellets. But once the pellets hit the wort, they expand about 10-fold. For example, a 4 inch by 6 inch bag can hold 5-6 ounces of dry pellets, but when the hops get wet the bag will only comfortably hold 3/4 of an ounce! One is advised to use the larger bag for bittering hops (whole or pellet).

Using Hop Extracts to Bitter Your Beer

Isomerized hop extracts are discussed in Chapter 5. These are pure alpha acids that have been pre-isomerized in a lab. You can add them in place of hops in the kettle, but it is recommended that if you do this, that you use the extracts for no more than 50% of the beer's bitterness and use real hops for the rest. The reason is that you get benefits from boiling the wort with real hops (like a better hot break and reduced surface tension) that you won't get with the extracts. Also, if you add the extracts to the wort, they will be subject to all of the fermentation losses described in Chapter 8. Therefore, isomerized hop extracts are best added post-fermentation, generally just prior to bottling or kegging. This way the losses will be minimized.

Make sure you get extracts that are calibrated to a known IBU or iso-alpha acid percentage so you will know how much to add to your beer. You should also try and get extracts made without toxic solvents. See Chapter 5 for more information.

The extract should come with instructions for use, but in general the procedure consists of stirring in the correct amount of extract in the priming tank (if you bottle) or adding to the serving/conditioning tank or keg. You can also use a procedure similar to the Taste-Titration Method described in Chapter 8 to figure out how much to add by taste. It consists mainly of adding small amounts (calibrated of course) to a glass of beer and tasting until you get the bitterness where you want it. Then scale up to the batch size to determine the amount to add.

Fixing a Beer That is Under-Bittered

What do you do if you taste a batch of beer and it doesn't have enough bitterness? If you've bottled it already, it's harder to fix. If you kegged the beer (or are a microbrewery) it's much easier.

The easiest way is to use the iso-alpha extracts

described above. Simply add the correct amount to the keg or serving tank and the beer will be fixed. This is probably the best reason for the microbrewer or homebrewer for using these extracts. (You can also add the extract to a pitcher of beer just before serving.)

A second method involves making a hop tea by boiling some hops in water for about an hour and adding it to the beer. The disadvantage of this method is that in order to keep the volume of water down so the beer doesn't get too diluted, you're going to use *a lot* of hops. Remember that hops are less efficiently utilized at high hopping rates. Use the formulas in Chapter 8 to figure out how many IBUs you'll get in the final boiled water. Just use the utilization and hop rate factors, and increase by about 20% for water vs. wort. Just remember to calculate your final IBUs by the dilution factor of your hop tea boil volume to the batch size.

If you have bottled your beer, you have three options. You can add some iso-alpha extract to a pitcher and pour the beer into it prior to serving. If you want the beer to be correct right of the bottle, you can carefully open all the bottles and gently pour them back into the bottling bucket. You want to do this carefully to avoid oxidation. Add the iso-alpha extract or hop tea and new priming sugar and rebottle. Lastly, you can make up a priming solution, let it cool, add iso-alpha extract to it. Now get a syringe or pipette (try your local lab supply) and open each bottle and inject the iso-alpha extract/priming solution into the bottle and recap. The priming solution volume has to be made so that it comes out to the right volume for the number of bottles you have, and the reason for the syringe or pipette is so that you can get a measured quantity into each bottle. In both cases, you'll want the priming solution to be a bit weaker than the first (especially in the second case) because the beer will retain some carbonation. It may not be worth all the effort. You can always cook with the beer, or claim to have invented a new style! (You were looking for an excuse to get that kegging system anyway!)

Fixing a Beer that is Over-Bittered

This is harder. If you are a microbrewer and have the excess capacity, brew another batch of beer that is under-bittered and blend the two. If you are homebrewer and keg your beer, you can do the same thing or you can dilute the beer with a commercial beer like Bud. Bud is neutral enough that it won't detract from your beer. Experiment with small amounts of the beers to get the ratio you like, then scale up to your batch size. If you bottled the beer, about the only thing you can do is carefully empty the beer into your bottling bucket, dilute with less-bittered beer, re-prime (lightly) and rebottle. Try to avoid oxidation as much as possible. You might consider adding a little ascorbate and/or using some of the oxygen absorbing bottle caps on the market. The growth of the yeast will also use up some of the oxygen. You could also dilute the beer at serving time by pouring the correct amount of the two beers together into a pitcher before serving.

Chapter 10 - Using Hops to Add Hop Character

Hop character is the term I like to describe the flavor that is caused by adding hops late in the boil. These additions are usually called *late hop additions, late kettle additions, late hopping* or *finish hopping*. I prefer the term finish hopping, so that's what I'll use (for the most part) in the remainder of this chapter. Hop character can also be imparted to the beer by use of the hop back. The hop back has been described in previous chapters, but in this chapter we will tell you how to use one to impart hop character to your beer.

What is Hop Character?

Hop character is very hard to describe in words. It is caused by the hop oils and not by the alpha acids. It has a very aromatic quality, but it is not the same as the aroma of fresh hops or the aroma imparted by dry hopping. If a beer has not been dry hopped, but has been liberally finish hopped, then the beer may have a decent hop nose, but again this aroma will be entirely different than a dry hop aroma. Hop character is really a combination of taste and smell, but the emphasis is on the taste. The aroma is different because a lot of the compounds that are retained

165

during dry hopping are lost when finish hopping, and the heat of the wort alters some of the compounds in the oil and changes their taste and aroma.

The qualities and intensity of the hop character will depend on many factors. Probably the most important is the amount and variety of the hop used. Each hop will impart a different hop character to the beer. The freshness of the hop is also important. One usually wants the freshest hops available, but a slight bit of aging may be beneficial with some hop varieties, particularly the "noble" varieties and their brew-alikes. The amount of oil contained in the hops is also important - the more oil the more intense the flavor will be for a given hop weight. The amount of time the hops are left in contact with the hot wort will also affect the intensity and the flavor - differing times will give different flavor profiles. Lastly, since we are dealing with short contact times, pellets are likely to be more efficient for finish hopping than whole hops, since the oils can get into the wort more readily.

Finish hopping not only gives the beer a unique character from the hops, but will also enhance the body and mouthfeel of the beer. Some brewers will question this statement, believing that all beer body comes from unfermentable dextrins from the malt. I used to believe this too. But adding some late hop essence (described later) to beer and doing side-by-side taste comparisons convinced me that finish hopping plays a large role in the perception of the beer's body.

Finish Hopping

The primary method used to get hop character in the beer is to add hops very late in the boil. Usually these times vary from 15 minutes before knockout (the end of the boil) to an addition right at knockout with some amount of time while the hops steep in the hot wort before it is cooled. There can be one addition or several. For example, in an American style hoppy pale ale, I like to add a portion of my finishing hops at around 10 minutes before knockout, and another amount right at knockout with about a 20 minute steeping time.

Since the finish hopping addition times are so short, very little isomerization of the alpha acids takes place. Any small amount formed will increase a beer's bitterness by a negligible amount, especially when post-boil losses are taken into account. So we don't generally need to worry about the bittering contributions from late hop additions. An exception might be for microbrewers that use a whirlpool separator where the agitation of the hops will increase the isomerization. Since the temperature at this time is well below boiling, the effect is likely to be minimal, however. The late hop character will tend to increase the perception of the beer's bitterness, even though it doesn't actually increase the beer's IBU rating. Pellets are likely to cause more bittering in this case than whole hops.

Choosing Hops for Finish Hopping

The obvious choice here is to use an aroma hop for finishing. There are some "dual purpose" hops that can be used for bittering as well as finishing. Examples are Centennial and Northern Brewer. There is no rule that says you can't use a bittering hop (like Chinook) for finishing, if that's what you like. I know a lot of brewers that use Chinook for just this purpose (some even dry hop with it), but it's not for me. *They* like their beers, and so do a lot of others, and that's what's important. If you have used an aroma hop for bittering, then you probably want to use that same hop for finishing, but again there's no rule that says you must. You can also use a single variety or a blend of varieties.

In the chapter on *Hop Varieties*, appropriate beer styles for each hop are suggested. For the aroma hops, the suggestions given there can apply to use as a bittering hop, but they are mainly for finish hopping and/or dry hopping.

Try and get the freshest hops possible for finish hopping. If you can find hops rated for oil content, that is a big plus. You can use the oil content to adjust your finish hop rate just like we used the alpha acid rating to adjust the bittering hop rate. This will be presented in more detail a bit later in the chapter.

Finish Hopping Schedules and Amounts

Once you have decided what hop or blend of hops you would like to use, you need to decide when to add them and how much.

You know that finishing hops are added near the end of the boil. The reason they are added near the end of the boil is due to the fact that the hop oils are what cause the effect we are striving for. Since the hop oils are very volatile, many of the oils' components (of which there are over 300), are lost almost immediately upon contact with the hot wort. Some take longer to evaporate than others. Depending on the length of time the hops are boiled, the hop character will be different because more or less of the hop oil compounds will be retained. Also, the heat changes some of the oil compounds, and the length of the heating affects the amount of the change.

When we use whole hops for finishing, it takes a certain amount of time for the oils to be extracted from the lupulin glands. With pellets, the oil has already been squeezed out and is available to go into the wort right away. (Some brewers believe that the quality of the hop oil is lessened or changed somehow in the pelletizing process. You need to decide for yourself. But I will emphasize again that your primary consideration for choosing pellets or whole hops should be how they behave physically in your brewing setup, not because of the minor differences in quality or extraction rates).

So as the hops remain in the boiling wort, the hop character continues to change. There has not been a lot of research done in the area of what the optimal time is, or what the differences are in the perceived hop character for different contact times.

My personal recommendation is to limit your *boil* contact time to 10 minutes or less. This will give you maximum effect and you will be assured that you get no extra bittering from your finishing additions. As a general rule, you can't really go wrong with a single addition at 5 minutes before knockout. You can vary the intensity of the hop character by varying the amount of the addition. If you want more hop flavor than aroma, add the hops at 10 minutes before knockout. If you want to emphasize the aroma, add them just before turning off the heat, cover and steep them for 20 minutes or so.

A lot will also depend on how you cool your wort. If you use an immersion chiller, the hops will be steeped pretty much automatically. If you don't want a lot of aroma, then add your hops at 10 minutes before knockout, since the covered steeping while chilling will retain a lot of the aroma compounds. If you want to emphasize the aroma, then your chilling cycle will pretty much do for the steeping, so no additional steeping is necessary. For those doing ice bath style cooling by putting the kettle in an ice bath, your cooling cycle is much longer and slower. Certainly no additional steeping time is necessary, and you may even want to consider using less hops. For those using counter-flow chillers, you'll have to gauge the amount of contact time for yourself and make adjustments accordingly. For example, if you get all your wort chilled in 5 minutes, then you might add some steeping time.

What quantity of hops should you add? It really depends on the oil content of the hops and the style of beer or the intensity of the effect you want. If you want a very light amount of hop character, try 1/2 ounce of hops. A medium amount would be around one ounce and a strong hop character would be 1 1/2 to 2 ounces. Depending on whether you want to emphasize the flavor or aroma, you can add them early, late or a split between the two for a balanced effect. These hop weights assume about 0.7-to 1% total oil content and a five gallon batch size. If your total oil content or batch size are different, you can adjust accordingly. If you don't know the oil content, you're really just winging it.

Oil Content Rating

If you know the oil content of your hops, this will also help you adjust the amount of the addition. Unlike IBUs and alpha acids, there hasn't been a lot of research in the area of finishing hopping as it relates to predicting hopping rates for various effects. Some researchers did propose an aroma unit (the AU). It is based on 22 of the hop oil components. It requires a high precision analysis of the hops using a gas chromatograph, and the AU for a given sample can change pretty drastically over time, in an unpredictable way. Thus, it really requires measuring the hops fairly often and isn't very practical for large scale brewers, let alone home and microbrewers. Because of the high costs involved with the measurements, I don't expect the AU to become a standard hop rating. Until we have something better, we will have to work with the total oil content, which is easily and cheaply measured by hop suppliers. According to one of the researchers involved in the AU project, total oil content rating, while not ideal, will get us about 80% there if you are using fresh hops.

Once you have arrived at a finishing hop schedule and amount you liked, assuming you kept good records and knew the oil content of the hops you used, you can now make adjustments to the amount of hops using the oil content as a guide. Let's say you were making a pale ale with Cascade and you finish hopped it by adding 1 ounce of hops at 5 minutes before knockout. The hops were really fresh and they had 1.3% oil content. Six months later you want to make the same recipe again, but now the hops you've just got in only have 0.8% oil content. (This could be due to losses from aging, or it could be a different lot, or both.) If you added the same 1 ounce of the new hops, you will get a lot less hop character than you had in the first beer.

To adjust the amount of hops based on the oil content rating, use the following formula:

$$\text{New Hop Amount} = \frac{\text{Original Oil Content}}{\text{New Oil Content}} * \text{Original Hop Amount}$$

where the original oil content and amount refers to the hops in the batch you liked the effect of, and the new oil content and amount refers to the new hops if they have differing oil contents. In our example, (1.3/0.8) * 1 = 1.625 ounces of the new hop. So to get the same amount of hop character in your beer as before, you'd now use 1.6 ounces of the newly arrived hops with 0.8% oil content.

This is only really valid if you use the same hop variety. If you switch hop varieties, you can use the formula to get you in the ballpark, but since the aroma qualities of the two hops will be different, so will the hop character in your beer, even if you adjust for oil content variations. It is likely to be close, however. And if the aroma varieties are similar (say Willamette vs. Fuggle or Mt. Hood vs. Liberty) it is likely to be close enough.

Also I should mention that this formula should be used only as a guideline, not a hard and fast "absolute" measurement. Why? Because some of hop oil compounds actually get "hoppier" as the hops age, so the oil content losses may not be exactly proportional to the "hoppiness" of the hop. This varies quite a bit depending on the hop variety and a host of other factors.

The Hop Back

Another way brewers get a late hop character in their beer is by use of the hop back. The hop back has been described a couple of times in this book already, but briefly it was originally a device that was intended to strain the hops out of the kettle. It also acted to filter some of the trub from the wort. Brewers discovered that if they loaded the hop back with some fresh hops before pouring the hot wort through it, that it imparted a unique hop character to the beer. It is somewhere between a late hop character and a dry hop effect. It tends more towards the late hop character than the dry hop effect.

The most famous widely available example of a beer that used a hop back was Sierra Nevada Pale Ale, known for its signature Cascade hop character and nose. But you'll notice that the previous sentence is in the past tense. This is because Sierra Nevada no longer uses the hop back. They have substituted a generous late hop addition with a 30 minute steep. The effect is nearly indistinguishable and is a lot less hassle.

There are currently no hop backs on the market for homebrewers. Microbrewers can have one made, and there are some "standards" available on that scale. You can make your own if you really want to try the hop back. But it requires that you be willing to siphon, pump or pour boiling hot wort, so it is definitely not for the novice brewer.

Hop backs will come in two styles: the open system and the closed system. The open system is the easiest of the two to put together. Basically it consists of a strainer that is large enough to hold at least 2-3 ounces of whole hops, plus the hops you used in the boil and any trub. You can use a large commercial strainer, add 2-3 ounces of fresh hops and pour or siphon the wort from your brew kettle through the strainer and into another kettle. The 1992 Special Issue of *Zymurgy* on Gadgets has plans for a hop back made out of the bottom of an old coffee urn, based on the open strainer principle. You can also use your lauter tun for the purpose. Listermann Manufacturing Company makes a mini-lauter tun that is also useful as a hop back. But I will caution you about pouring hot wort. Be careful! It is best handled as two or three person operation.

The closed design basically works like an in-line filter. The same special issue of *Zymurgy* has another do-it-yourself hop back design based on a mason jar that uses the closed system principle. The advantage of the closed system is that more of the hop oils will be retained and therefore the effect will be more intense. It is a little harder to build and maintain. The mini-lauter tun referred to above can also be converted to a semi-closed system by drilling a hole in the bucket lid and installing an appropriate sized hose fitting or force-fitting the hose in the hole.

Both systems require that you cool the wort quickly after being run through the hop back, and that means you'll need to use a counter-flow chiller. If you use one of these, you can just hook up the hop back in-line between your kettle and the chiller.

Is it worth all the trouble? My opinion is not really. You can do like Sierra Nevada does and add hops at knockout and let them steep, covered, for 20-30 minutes before chilling, or while you're chilling if you use an immersion method. Just don't be afraid to use a lot of hops.

Late Hop Essences

Late Hop Essences have been described in the chapter on *Hop Products*. They are fractions of the hop oil that are said to be responsible for late hop effects. They come in two varieties, a Spicy and a Floral. While they are very interesting products in their own right, they just aren't quite the same as real late hopping. Probably because late hopping provides some aroma effects and the late hop essences only provide taste effects. Even so, they are worth a try. The Spicy fraction can really give your beer a boost in its apparent body and mouthfeel. The Floral fraction is hard to describe. It gives the beer a floral taste, not an aroma. The effect is unique and quite pleasant. The two fractions can be used individually or in various combinations for a wide range of effects. Their most useful purpose is patching a beer that didn't have enough late hopping.

It is important to get a calibrated product and also one that has been derived from hop oils that have been extracted without toxic solvents. See the chapter on *Hop Products* for more information.

Beer Styles and Hop Character

The following table will give you some recommendations as to whether or not it is appropriate for a particular beer style to have hop character, and if so, how intense the effect should be. This table should be used only as a guide. Feel free to experiment and add hop character to any style you wish. This is, after all, how we get new styles.

Using Hops to Add Hop Character

Style	Hop Character
Barley Wine	Medium-Strong
Belgian Brown Ale	None-Light
Belgian White (Wit)	None
Belgian Trappist House and Doubles	Light-Medium
Belgian Trappist Triples	Light-Medium
Saison	Medium
Lambics	None
English Mild	Light
English Brown Ale	Light
American Brown Ale	None-Medium
English Pale Ale	Medium-Strong
India Pale Ale (IPA)	Strong
American Pale Ale	Medium-Strong
English Ordinary Bitter	Medium
English Extra Special Bitter (ESB)	Medium-Strong
Scottish Light Ale	None-Light
Scottish Heavy	None-Light
Scottish Export	None-Light
Robust Porter	Medium
Brown Porter	Medium
English Old/Strong Ale	Light
Scotch Strong Ale	None-Light
Dry Stout	None-Light
Sweet (Cream) Stout	None
Imperial Stout	Light-Medium
German Bock	Light
Helles (Pale) Bock	None-Light
Dopplebock	Light
Dunkel	None-Light
American Dark Lager	None
Dortmund/Export	Medium
Munich Helles	Light
Classic Pilsner	Medium-Strong
German Pilsner	Medium-Strong
American "Lite" Lager	None
American Lager	None
American Premium Lager	None
American "Dry" Lager	None
American "Microbrewed" Lager	Medium-Strong
American Wheat Beer	None
Vienna	None-Light
Marzen/Octoberfest	None-Light

175

```
Alt Beer ................................................................ Medium
Kolsch................................................................ Light
Cream Ale ........................................................... None
Fruit Ale ............................................................. None
Herbed and Spiced Beer ..................................... Varies a lot
Smoked Beer ....................................................... Light
Anchor Steam Style * .......................................... Medium-Strong
Berliner Weisse .................................................. None
German Weizen and Hefe-weizen ....................... None
```

* Steam Beer is a trademark of Anchor Brewing and may not be used by any brewery for commercial purposes. It is also known as California Common Beer.

Fixing a Beer with Too Little Hop Character

If you expected to get hop character in your beer and you didn't get enough, you have a couple of options. You can add some Late Hop Essence that was described earlier. You can brew up some "late hop tea" and add that. Do this by bringing about a quart of water to a boil and add aroma hops. Boil about 5 minutes. Cover and let steep for as long as you want, up to about 30 minutes. Strain the hops and add the hot tea to the beer, letting the beer cool the tea. If you cool the tea first, you risk it getting a lot of oxygen in it, and now is not when you want oxygen in your beer. You can combine this with the priming step if you have discovered the problem before bottling. If you have already bottled, see the previous chapter's sections on fixing an under-bittered beer for suggestions, but substitute the late hop tea described here for the bitter tea described in that section.

Chapter 11 - Using Hops to Add Hop Aroma

In the last chapter we discussed *late hop character*. Late hop character is both a flavor and an aroma sensation, and is caused by the hop oils. In this chapter we're going to discuss *hop aroma*. The hop aroma we're going to talk about now is not the same aroma you get from late hopping. We're talking about a fresh hop aroma, as close as we can get to smelling the hops by themselves. This aroma is caused by hop oils as well, but since the hop oils will not be heated in the process, the aroma resembles that of fresh hops.

There are a few ways to get the aroma of fresh hops in your beer, but the most common way is through a process known as *dry hopping*. It can also be accomplished by adding hop oils directly to the beer, and by making a hop tea.

What is Dry Hopping?

Dry Hopping. Ask two brewing experts what that phrase means and you'll get three opinions. Try looking it up in the available literature and you'll get a wide variety of definitions and very little consensus amongst authors. On the other hand, a good many recipes call for a certain amount of hops to be "dry hopped" with no explanation of the method.

If we examine the homebrewing literature and try to put together a definition of dry hopping that accommodates all of the author's individual definitions, we come up with a definition that would read like this: *Dry hopping is the process of adding hops to the beer at a point anywhere from after the kettle boil up to and including the bottling process.* Now that is a *very* long period of time consisting of many brewing stages. Obviously adding the hops just after turning off the heat will have a completely different effect than adding the same amount of hops during the secondary fermentation. In this chapter, we'll examine the various "options" for when to add the hops, and examine their relative merits and demerits.

Dry hopping is done with one main purpose: to get the aroma of fresh hops to come through in the beer. But there is another side-benefit from dry hopping. Fritz Maytag of Anchor Brewing says they have discovered that dry hopping has amazing preservative effects on the beer. People are still enjoying bottles of dry hopped Anchor "Our Special Ale" that are almost 20 years old!

Traditional Dry Hopping

Dry hopping has been practiced for centuries in England, and was sometimes called *raw hopping*. No one is quite sure where the term dry hopping came from, but my theory follows: In olden times it was quite common to reuse the kettle hops a few times in successive boils before discarding them. These hops would have been "wet" (even though some fresh, dry hops would have been added as well). In contrast, the hops added in the later conditioning stages were always fresh and dry.

In England, cask conditioned ales will typically get

fresh "dry" hops added along with finings and priming sugar (or krausen) when the beer is racked from the primary fermenter into the cask. This is the true, traditional dry hopping method. The cask is then left to "condition" for 7 to 14 days at around 55° F. The oil from the hops is slowly extracted from the hops and disseminated throughout the beer.

If you use a "kegging" system instead of bottle conditioning your beer, you can follow essentially the same procedure as they do in England. Add your fresh aroma hops to the tank along with the priming sugar and optionally, finings. If you force carbonate the beer, you'll still have to let the beer sit with the hops for one to two weeks to allow the hop oil to be extracted into the beer. You can add the hops loose or tie them in a hop bag to make clean-up easier and remove any potential for clogging your beer lines. You can tie the bag to the bottom of the dip tube to keep the hops immersed in the beer (they tend to float to the top) or can try wedging the hop bag in-between the dip tube and the wall of the keg. A common method is to add some weights to the bag with the hops. Use glass marbles, a piece of stainless steel or some other easily cleaned and sterilized weight. Ceramic (not metal) "pie weights" are available in most kitchen stores. Just be sure not to use lead fishing weights! You will be surprised at the amount of weight it takes. When devising your own weight system, test it first in a bucket.

There are some fine mesh cotton bags on the market that allow you to use pellets. The advantage of pellets is that the hop oils have already been liberated from the lupulin glands and will get into the beer faster than whole hops, and probably with more efficiency. This means you can use less. As has been mentioned before, some brewers believe that some "magic" is missing from the aroma of pellet hops compared to whole hops.

179

Whole hops should also be used in a bag, but they don't necessarily have to be. They will float to the top of your beer and won't clog the pickup tube. The disadvantage is that your extraction rate will be slightly poorer because a good deal of the hop surface area will not be in the beer. I like to use whole hops in a weighted bag in the serving keg because the hop aroma seems to keep coming out of them, and it takes me a few months to finish a 5 gallon keg.

The advantage of traditional dry hopping is that there is no place for the hop aroma to go but into the beer. The only disadvantage is the time you have to wait before you can drink the beer. The time will vary with the temperature, but one to two weeks is a good average. The lower the temperature, the longer it will take to extract the hop aroma. The only problem is that if you don't have a kegging system, you need to do something else to get hop aroma into your beer.

"Fermentation" Dry Hopping

Fortunately, there are alternatives to traditional dry hopping during the conditioning stage of the beer. The most widely practiced alternative is dry hopping by adding fresh hops to the fermenter. Now there are many points at which you could add the hops during fermentation. They all have their pros and cons. Let's examine each possibility.

Adding Hops to the Primary

Some books recommend that to dry hop you should add your hops to the primary fermenter as soon as the wort is cooled to about 75° F, or about the same time as you pitch the yeast. This can work, but there are some good reasons to wait a bit.

Hops are not a sterile product. They contain bacteria and wild yeast. In a study done at UC Davis, it was determined that the microbiological risks from dry hopping were essentially non-existent. The fermentation process swamped any attempt of the yeast or bacteria on the hops to get established. *However*, this assumes a well maintained and vigorous yeast starter as would be used by a commercial brewery or microbrewery. Not all homebrewers can be guaranteed a good, fast fermentation start, especially if you're using liquid yeast and not using a secondary starter step beyond the starter in the pouch. Therefore, there is some risk of contamination by the hops if they are added at pitching time. But there is no need to take an unnecessary risk.

Besides, much of the hop aroma will be scrubbed out of the wort by the vigorous action of the primary fermentation. Great volumes of CO_2 are given off and it will carry the hop aroma along with it. The hops will only be in contact with the beer for a short amount of time if you rack into a secondary. To compensate for all these losses, you'll have to add a lot of hops, which is costly and wasteful. I can't think of any advantages to adding hops along with the yeast. Given all the disadvantages, there's no reason to do it.

Adding Hops to the Secondary

Dry hopping by adding fresh hops to the secondary fermentation stage is the next best alternative to traditional dry hopping in the serving or conditioning keg. There is virtually no risk of contamination since the established yeast growth, alcohol and lower pH will inhibit any yeast or bacteria introduced with the hops. Since much less CO_2 is being given off, less hop aroma will be lost to the atmosphere so you'll need less hops.

Using Hops

To dry hop your beer in the secondary, add the hops to the secondary container before racking the beer into it. The beer should be left on the hops for around two weeks, depending on the temperature (colder=longer). You can add loose whole hops, the hops in a weighted hop bag as described earlier, or hop pellets.

Note that even if you use only one fermentation vessel (as is common with ales and those using plastic bucket fermenters) and don't rack the beer into a "secondary" vessel, your beer still goes through primary and secondary fermentation stages. You just add the hops at the beginning of the secondary stage (at the time you would have racked into the secondary, if you did that). The primary stage is characterized by heavy activity, lots of bubbling and usually a lot of foam on the top of the beer. The secondary stage starts as fermentation slows down and is characterized by the foam head dropping back and bubbling of the airlock slowing down.

If you are using a plastic bucket type fermenter, open the top and add your hops. If you are adding loose whole hops or pellets, stir them in as best you can with a sanitized spoon, but be careful not to oxidize your beer. Then replace the top and the airlock. If you are using the weighted hop bag approach, just drop the bag in (gently) and replace the top. If you are using a carboy, pellets are easily fed in through the top. Whole, loose hops are bit more of a problem. Make yourself a wide funnel out of a clean sheet of paper. You'll still probably need to push the hops in with a sanitized pusher of some sort (your racking tube would be a good, handy candidate).

When adding hops in a weighted hop bag to an empty carboy (before racking the beer over), I advise you to lay the carboy on its side, insert the hop bag and weight and let them slide down the shoulder. Then slowly upright the carboy. If you just drop the weight in, you risk breaking the carboy. If the carboy is full of beer (as in the single vessel example above), then the beer will cushion the blow, so don't bother trying to tilt the carboy.

Using Hop Oil to Add Hop Aroma

Hop oils and iso-alpha extracts have been described in the chapter on *Hop Products*. Hop iso-alpha extract is of no concern to us because that is used for bittering, not aroma. Hop oil, on the other hand, would appear to be exactly what we want. Hop oil is extracted from the hops by one of three methods: Steam distillation, solvent extraction and low temperature CO_2 extraction.

Because of the temperatures involved, steam distillation changes the character of the hop oil from the fresh hop aroma into a cooked hop aroma, not unlike the effect of late addition hops. Adding this product to our beer might eliminate the need to add hops late in the boil, but won't accomplish our goal of fresh hop aroma.

Solvent extracted hop oil is made by immersing the hops in a strong toxic solvent - either hexane or methylene chloride - to extract the oil. The solvent is removed from the oil by heating the mixture, which changes the aroma as in steam distillation and many of the aromatic compounds are evaporated with the solvent. Also, there are concerns that some traces of the solvent remain. I don't want any toxic solvents in my beer, and I assume you don't want any in yours either.

A recent innovation is the extraction of hop oil by using high pressure, low temperature liquid CO_2. Since there are no high temperatures involved, the hop aroma stays intact. There are no toxic solvents involved and CO_2 is a natural part of beer anyway. CO_2 extracted hop oil is definitely the one to use!

The advantages of CO_2 extracted hop oil are many: You use the hop oil by mixing it in the raw beer during the priming step, just before bottling (or kegging). This means that most of the hop aroma will be trapped in the bottle/ keg until it's time to drink. This is very close to (maybe even better than) traditional dry hopping in the cask. In fact, a lot of commercial breweries in England do just this. There is no risk from infection. Another advantage of hop oil is that the aromatic qualities can be blended from different hop varieties and batches to achieve consistent aromatic qualities from year to year. And the effect is instant. No waiting one to two weeks for the hop aroma to get into the beer.

There *are* a few disadvantages. The choice of aromas is limited. You can't just walk into the local homebrew store and ask for Cascade or Fuggle or whatever you like. You must usually settle for a blend, but sometimes specific "pure" varietal hop oils are available. While the blending described as an advantage above means consistency, it also means there is no identifiable varietal characteristic. Hop oil used to be very hard to use in its pure form. The arrival of diluted formulations on the market has eliminated that disadvantage, however. For more information, see Chapter 5 on *Hop Products*.

To use hop oil to get hop aroma in your beer, you simply add the hop oil at bottling or kegging time. The biggest issue is how much to add. If the product is a formulation, it may come with instructions on how to add a small amount to a glass of similar beer to determine how much to add to the full batch. This, of course, implies that you have a calibrated product. The dosage is extremely important! If you add too little, the effect will not be noticeable. If you add too much, the effect will be like someone dumped cheap perfume into your beer. The "just right" region is very small, so I urge you to experiment as per the instructions with the hop oil. If they don't come with instructions or the product isn't calibrated, your hop oil experience is likely to be dissatisfying.

Hop Tea

If you like the idea of adding hop aroma just before bottling (or kegging) so it stays trapped until it's time to drink the beer, but you don't want to use hop oil, you can give "hop tea" a try. This has been suggested by other authors, but they usually tell you to *boil* the hops. We already know that boiling will destroy the fresh hop aroma so that's out. A better method was suggested to me by Lynne O'Connor, owner of St. Patrick's of Texas. She recommends steeping 1 to 2 oz. of hops in hot water and then adding that to the priming tank with the sugar just prior to bottling. You could combine the hop tea and sugar priming steps by first bringing the water to a boil, dissolving the sugar and letting it cool (covered) to around 150° F. Stir in the hops, cover and let steep for 30 minutes to an hour while the mixture cools. Strain the liquid into the beer and mix well. You'll want to use whole hops as opposed to pellets unless you've got a *very* fine strainer. It's also important to remember not to boil the hops. This will destroy the hop aroma.

Bottle Hopping

If you bottle condition your beer, you can experiment with adding a fresh whole hop cone to the bottle just before filling. I have only achieved limited success with this method and is not worth the effort in my opinion. But here are some tips: Use the biggest, freshest cones you can find. Trap the cone at the bottom of the bottle with the bottle filler so it doesn't float to the top while filling. And when pouring, expect to get some yeast in the glass since the cone will disturb it during pouring. But have fun!

How Much and What Kind of Hops to Use

This is a matter of personal taste. It is my opinion that most recipes call for far too little aroma/finishing hops and even less dry hops. Check it out yourself by looking at the recipes in various issues of *Zymurgy*. Compare the amount of hops used with the judge's comments on hop aroma. You'll find that most recipes using around 1/2 an ounce of aroma and/or dry hops (per five gallons) got comments like "Could use more hop aroma" or "Not much hop aroma" whereas those using an ounce or more of finishing and/or dry hops got good hop aroma comments. The conclusion is to use more hops than you think (it's better to err on the high side). A lot will depend on the freshness of the hops and the method you use, but between 1 and 2 ounces is a good place to start. Also important is the style of beer. A following section will list those beer styles for which dry hopping is appropriate, but the lighter the beer flavor, the less aroma hops you need and conversely the heavier the beer the more hops you need. The oil content of the hops is also very important (see the next section for more information).

As for what kind of hops to use, well they don't separate hops into bittering and aroma varieties for no particular reason! Obviously you're going to use an aroma variety. You might start by buying a few ounces of many different aroma varieties and sniffing them. (Any you don't like the aroma of can always be used for bittering since the aroma will be boiled off.) Get them as fresh as you can and make sure your hop supplier uses oxygen barrier bags. The test is to see if you can smell the hops through the sealed bag. If you can, then it's not an oxygen barrier bag. Buy from another supplier.

I can't emphasize enough that for dry hopping you need to have extremely fresh hops. Freshness is everything. If you can smell any off aromas, don't use those hops unless you want that aroma in your beer.

Oil Content Rating

If you know the oil content of your hops, this will also help you adjust the amount of the addition. Unlike IBUs and alpha acids, there hasn't been a lot of research in the area of dry hopping as it relates to predicting hopping rates. No one even knows what percentage of hop oil introduced as hops ends up in the beer. Anyway, you're going to have to experiment to find a hop rate that you like for a given style.

The method and considerations for adjusting hopping rates using the oil content as a guide have been discussed in the previous chapter. Rather than repeat the information here, refer to the similarly named section there. You'll just be adjusting the dry hop amount instead of the finishing hop amount described there.

Dry Hopping Problems

Sometimes homebrewers will report a great increase in bitterness after dry hopping. This is not to be confused with the slight enhancement of the beer's perceived bitterness due to the hop oils. We're talking really undrinkable levels of bitterness. I have not ever tasted one of these beers myself, nor have I ever met an *experienced* brewer that had this happen.

Dry hopping will sometimes cause an increase in a beer's *astringency*, which can often be mistaken for bitterness. This has not happened to any of my beers, but I have tasted beers where this has been the case. In every case however, this astringency vanished in a few weeks. No one knows for sure why this happens, but my theory is that it is caused by the hop tannins. Eventually these tannins drop out or combine with other compounds in the beer and lose their astringency.

It is possible that some of these brewers used "pre-isomerized" or "stabilized" hop pellets where a good portion of the alpha acids have been converted into iso-alpha acids. If this were the case, then these pellets would indeed bitter the beer without boiling. Normal hops just can't accomplish this feat.

If you keg the beer and dry hop in the serving keg, and like me can't wait a week or two for the hop aroma to get into the beer, you may notice that your beer is very "grassy" tasting. This too will pass with time.

Lastly, dry hopping in the secondary may cause fermentation to become visibly more active again, or it may simply have appeared to do so. Stirring in the hops may have the effect of rousing the yeast, and that may cause fermentation to kick into a higher gear for a while. Usually this is simply more CO_2 being released from the beer, the hops becoming bubble nucleation sites. In either case, it is nothing to worry about and in fact has the advantage of purging any oxygen you may have introduced.

Microbiological Risks of Dry Hopping

We covered this earlier in the chapter, but it bears repeating. If you dry hop in the secondary or later, there is virtually *no* risk of contaminating your beer by dry hopping. The alcohol content and low pH of the beer after the primary fermentation keeps anything that normally lives on fresh hops from getting going. Now many brewers will not agree with this. But I have never seen a documented case of contamination that was proved to be caused by dry hopping. I recently talked to a brewer that made a contaminated batch, and was convinced it came from the dry hopping he had done. He claimed not to have done anything different than in previous batches, except for dry hopping. After about 20 minutes of going through all of his procedures, he finally admitted that his prior three batches (which weren't dry hopped) were contaminated as well!

If you are really paranoid, you can soak the hops in some 100 proof vodka or Everclear for a few minutes. Then add the hops and the liquid to the beer.

Beer Styles and Dry Hopping

Not every classic beer style has a fresh hop or dry hop aroma. Until a very few years ago, dry hopping was limited to cask conditioned ales from England. And even dry hopping in those ales had diminished to the point where you really couldn't tell that the beer had been dry hopped at all. Fritz Maytag at Anchor Brewing is single-handedly responsible for the revival of dry hopping in this country and just might be responsible for an increase of the levels used in England.

Using Hops

It started when Fritz decided to make a traditional English Pale Ale. He journeyed to England and visited the major brewers. Most were still practicing dry hopping, but they were using such small amounts in each cask that it hardly mattered. He thought they were mainly doing it out of a sense of tradition rather than for any aroma effect.

It didn't always used to be that way! In the late 1800s, India Pale Ale was heavily dry hopped. To relate the amount they used to our common five gallon batches, they used around 2.5 ounces of hops in five gallons. Fritz found the English brewers using about a tenth of that amount.

Needless to say, Anchor's first Liberty Ale was heavily dry hopped, and remains so today. The exact amount remains a secret, but it is around 2 ozs in five gallons. Cascade is used exclusively. If you get a fresh bottle of Anchor Liberty Ale, it is one of the finest examples of a dry-hopped ale in existence. If you can get a glass from a fresh keg, or better yet at the brewery, wow! If you're a hophead like me, you'll be in hop-heaven (forgive the pun).

No one questions Fritz's and Anchor's role in starting the microbrewery revolution. But we should also thank him for bringing back beers where fresh hop aroma was important (and evident!).

Today, many brewers are experimenting with adding fresh hop aroma to beer styles that never had it before. I invite you to do the same. Even so, there are some styles where dry hopping would obviously be appropriate, and others where it would not. Before we get to the list, I should mention that beers that are dry hopped are usually heavily finish hopped as well. The two flavors compliment each other. So while it is not unusual to have a beer that is just finish hopped and not dry hopped, it would be highly unusual to find a beer that has been dry hopped but not finish hopped.

Style	Dry Hop?
Barley Wine	Yes
Belgian Brown Ale	No
Belgian White (Wit)	No
Belgian Trappist House and Doubles	No
Belgian Trappist Triples	No
Saison	No
Lambics	No
English Mild	No
English Brown Ale	No
American Brown Ale	Sometimes
English Pale Ale	Yes
India Pale Ale (IPA)	Yes
American Pale Ale	Yes
English Ordinary Bitter	No
English Extra Special Bitter (ESB)	Optional
Scottish Light Ale	No
Scottish Heavy	No
Scottish Export	No
Robust Porter	No
Brown Porter	No
English Old/Strong Ale	No
Scotch Strong Ale	No
Dry Stout	No
Sweet (Cream) Stout	No
Imperial Stout	No
German Bock	No
Helles (Pale) Bock	No
Dopplebock	No
Dunkel	No
American Dark Lager	No
Dortmund/Export	No
Munich Helles	No
Classic Pilsner	No
German Pilsner	No
American "Lite" Lager	No
American Lager	No
American Premium Lager	No
American Microbrewed Lager	Sometimes
American "Dry" Lager	No
American Wheat Beer	No
Vienna	No
Marzen/Octoberfest	No

Alt Beer .... No
Kolsch.. No
Cream Ale .... No
Fruit Ale .... No
Herbed and Spiced Beer .... Sometimes
Smoked Beer .... No
Anchor Steam Style * .... No
Berliner Weisse .... No
German Weizen and Hefe-weizen .... No

* Steam Beer is a trademark of Anchor Brewing and may not be used by any brewery for commercial purposes. It is also known as California Common Beer.

Summary of Dry Hopping Recommendations

Always dry hop in the secondary or later. Never dry hop in the primary. (If you use just one fermentation vessel, wait until the primary stages of fermentation are over.) If you keg your beer, dry hopping in the serving keg is the best place to do it. If you are a microbrewer, the conditioning tank is the best place. I recommend the use of a hop bag and weight. This keeps the hops suspended in the beer, and this promotes better extraction of the hop oils. If you use oil content rated hops, you will be in a better position to get repeatability from your dry hopping. If you dry hop, don't forget to finish hop as well. It is OK to finish hop without dry hopping, but generally not the other way around. Remember to get the freshest hops you can. Lastly, remember that dry hopping will not impart any bitterness to the beer. Most flavor problems with dry hopping stem from the fact that you're drinking the beer too early. Time will cure them. If you're the impatient type, try hop oils for an instant dry hop effect.

Chapter 12 - Growing Your Own Hops

Originally I was not going to include a chapter on growing hops, mainly because I don't know a lot about it. But a lot of you asked that information be included, and Dave Wills of Freshops agreed to write it. Most of what follows was written by Dave. Dave has been one of the premier suppliers of hop rhizomes (and whole hops) to the homebrewer and home hop farmer. Most of the rhizomes you see offered for sale each spring come from Dave. If you want to give hop growing a try, there is no better source for rhizomes or practical growing information (see the Freshops ad in the back of the book). I am very pleased to have Dave as a contributor to this book. His words follow.

Hop Gardening

The hop (*Humulus lupulus*) is a hardy, perennial plant which produces annual vines from a permanent root stock (crown). Vines may grow up to 25 feet in a single season but will die back to the crown each fall. In addition to the true roots and aerial vine, the crown also produces underground stems called the *rhizomes*. Rhizomes resemble roots but possess numerous buds and are used for vegetative propagation. Thus propagated, all plants of a given variety are genetically identical. The rhizome is the part of the plant that you buy in order to grow your own hops.

Hops are dioecious, which means they have separate male and female plants. Only the female produces the flowers that are used for brewing or medicinal purposes. Male plants have no commercial value but are used to pollinate females. Pollination stimulates higher yields by increasing cone size and seed set, but because brewers prefer seedless hops, males are only grown with otherwise poor yielding female varieties. Hop seed from a pollinated female is only planted when a cross between the male and female is desired to obtain a new variety.

Hops are native to the temperate zones of the northern hemisphere. They are found wild in western Europe, Asia and certain parts of North America. Commercial hops are generally grown between the 30th and 50th parallel north or south latitude and at various altitudes. Hops are very sensitive to short days and poor yields result at latitudes too close to the equator. Commercial hop production occurs in these countries: Argentina, Australia, Austria, Belgium, Bulgaria, Canada, China, Czechoslovakia, France, Germany, Great Britain, Hungary, India, Ireland, Japan, North Korea, South Korea, New Zealand, Poland, Portugal, Rumania, Russia, Serbia, Slovakia, Slovenia, South Africa, Spain, Switzerland, Turkey, and the United States. Therefore the ability to grow hops is usually not limited by your location on earth (within the defined latitudes). The health of the vine is more dependent on the growers ability to provide proper growing conditions and care. Under good conditions, hops are a prolific vine, will produce from 1/2- 2 pounds of dried flowers per plant, and will be a joy to grow and utilize.

Growth Cycle

When referring to hops, I am from here on referring to the female of the species. Being a perennial, the hop lays dormant during winter and is rather unaffected by freezing temperatures. The times when the annual vines break ground, when they flower and when they die back are determined by local temperature and day length. The vines will not break ground until soil temperatures have risen to the point where most spring flowers appear. A minimum of 120 frost free days are required for the hop to fully ripen a crop of flowers. Once out of the ground, the vines need to be supported off of the ground. Vegetative growth continues until approximately mid-July when most hops are either past bloom or in full bloom depending upon location and variety. At this "burr" stage the flower is approximately 1/4 inch in diameter and is composed of many florets whose *styles* give it a spiny appearance. This is when the flower is receptive to pollen and if males are present, wind borne pollen will fertilize the female flower and result in a seeded female hop cone. Regardless of pollination, the styles eventually fall off and miniature petals grow which eventually result in a cone-like structure which becomes the final form of the hop flower. Most female flowers develop and ripen predominately between mid-August and mid-September depending on location and variety. Earlier flowers can and will occur but this occurrence is highly variable based upon location, weather, and cultural practices. Commercial growers actually delay flowering by removing the earliest vines in the spring in order to enhance regrowth and encourage a higher yield of flowers. After the flowers ripen, the vine will continue to build reserves until it totally dies back with the first freezes of Fall.

Hop hills are covered with lime which will help condition the soil and raise the pH. Photo courtesy of Dave Wills.

Soil Preparation

Because hops can produce such a large vine in a matter of months, they will use a large amount of solar energy, water and nutrients. Hops prefer full sun and rich soil, preferably light textured, well drained soil with a pH of 5.5-8.0. If drainage is a problem, small mounds can be built using surrounding top soil mixed with organic matter. That is not to say that the hop will not grow under less than optimum conditions, only that the vines will be smaller. Because the hop is a perennial, it's not a bad idea to dig holes about one foot deep so that some manure and other slow release organic fertilizers can be mixed with your soil and replaced into the hole so the nutrients are in the root zone. After obtaining your rhizomes, keep them slightly moist in a plastic bag and stored in the refrigerator until planting. This will keep them from sprouting prematurely. Rhizomes should be planted vertically with the bud pointing up or horizontally in a shallow trench about 1" below the soil surface. First year " baby" hops have a minimal root system and require frequent short waterings much like any baby plant, but do not drown them with too much water. Mulching the soil surface with some organic matter works wonders in conserving moisture as well as helping to control weeds. Once the hop is established after the first season, less frequent deep watering is best, preferably with drip irrigation. Try not to soak the vine and leaves during watering, as that will sometimes encourage diseases. Each Spring apply a hardy dose of manure as a top dressing or fertilize with a balanced chemical fertilizer that is recommended for garden vegetables.

Spacing and Support

In a commercial hop yard, space between plants varies from country to country and is mainly based on the need to have enough room to allow tractors to get between the rows. In the United States, hops are grown on a 7' by 7' grid with an 18 foot tall trellis. In a home garden, the main concern is just to get the vines off the ground and possibly to keep different varieties from getting tangled up with each other. Plant mixed varieties at least 5 ft. apart. Identical varieties can be as close as 3 ft. if you don't have much room. Hops mainly grow up if they can, then lateral sidearms extend off of the nodes of the main vine. Hops don't have to be grown on an 18' trellis. Some of the less vigorous varieties will yield more if they are limited to more like 12'-15'. Actually just about anything over 6 feet will work, the vine will just become bushier. The vines are easiest to grow and deal with if they are trained onto strong twine. This twine can be supported by a trellis wire, pole, tree branch or building. Small diameter poles, lattice and chain link fence also work but require more hand labor. Keep in mind that the vine does die back each Fall. In the first year vines can be established with a 6 foot stake.

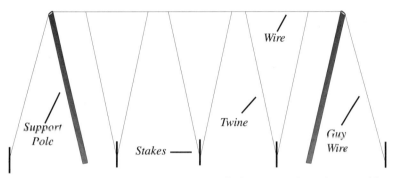

Typical Hop Trellis. End poles are installed at an angle and secured by guy-wires. Note there are two twines per hop plant/hill. Height should be 12-18 feet.

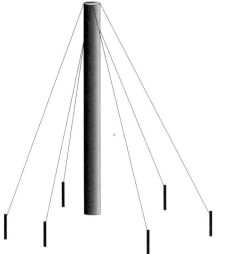

Tent Training - Multiple twines around a single pole.

If space is a problem, you can use your house as support.
Photo courtesy of Dave Wills.

Commercial hop farmers do not train up the first shoots of spring but prune them off mechanically. Hardier shoots are trained onto the string about 4 weeks later (early to mid May in Oregon). Only 2-3 vines should be trained onto each string with 2 strings per plant. All subsequent vines, (which can be extensive with older plants) should be cut off. Vines are ready to be trained when they are about 12" long and must be gently wrapped clockwise onto the string without kinking. Once trained, the vine will take care of itself unless you want the vine to grow horizontally, in which case this must be done manually.

Harvest

Because most hops are produced out of reach from the ground, it is safest to lower the vines in order to pick the hops. The harvest date varies with variety and location but

At harvest time the vine should be lowered to the ground for picking. If you can design your support wire to be lowered, that is the easiest method, but you can also cut the vine at the top as shown here. Note the orchard ladder. Photo courtesy of Dave Wills.

will become evident as you gain experience as a hop grower. At maturity, the hop aroma is at its strongest and is measured by crushing a cone and smelling it. The yellow lupulin glands in the cone become much more evident and plump looking when magnified. The cone will develop a drier, papery feel and in some varieties a lighter color as it matures. Some browning of the lower bracts is a good sign of ripeness. Squeeze the cones as they develop and you will notice they become more light and resilient rather than green and hard. The actual picking is self explanatory and this is where you want the flower cones, not the leaves. I don't know why raw hop cones are occasionally called leaf hops, when the idea is to not pick the leaves.

As was mentioned earlier, harvest will be easier if you can lower the entire vine to the ground for picking. This can be done if you can design your trellis support wire to be lowered. If that is not practical, the vines can be cut at the top and bottom. Lastly you can pick the cones from the vine "up in the air". In any case, you may want to invest in an orchard ladder. This is a three-legged ladder designed especially for working on tall trees and vines. Not only are they cheaper than a conventional step ladder of the same height, but the single leg makes it easier to set the ladder close to the base of the vines.

Drying

Drying can be done in a food dehydrator, custom made hop dryer, well vented oven, or air dried. If you use heat, the temperature should not exceed 140 degrees F or even lower if the airflow through the hops is low. Cooler temperatures take longer but a higher quality hop is obtained. Under dry weather conditions, I suggest using a window screen, setting it up in a wind protected area elevated on each end. Spread the hops as shallow as possible and fluff daily so moist inner cones are brought to the outside of the pile. If the weather is dry and the pile is not too thick they will dry in about three days. A high moisture content in the cones will adversely affect storageability and recipe formulation (since your weight will be incorrect). The hops are dry when the inner stem of the cone (strig) is brittle and breaks rather than bends. The strig takes much longer to dry than the bracts, so be patient. Pack the hops in an air tight container and store in a freezer until used. I can't emphasize enough to make sure your hops are dry before freezing them.

Diseases and Pests

Downy Mildew: *Pseudoperonospora humuli*

The primary disease in hops grown in the US is downy mildew. Because it is specific to hops, the disease may or may not be a problem where you are located. The disease first appears in the spring when some of the shoots develop into "basal spikes". The spikes are characterized by a stunted form, pale down-curled leaves, silvery upper surface and the underside of the leaf turns black. Once the shoot develops into a spike it will not continue to grow and should be removed as it is now a source of infection for other parts of this plant as well as other plants. There must be moisture on the leaves in order for the wind-borne spores to germinate. This is why it is a good idea to not sprinkle irrigate. Lower leaves are also often removed by hop growers as they create a damp area around the basal spikes ideal for spreading the disease. Downy mildew can be controlled by spraying a copper fungicide such as Kocide 101, but repeated applications may be necessary as rain will wash off the fungicide. Systemic fungicides such a Ridomil and Aliette provide longer protection but may not be available to home gardeners. Hopefully this disease is not a problem in your area, so don't worry about it until the spikes appear.

Powdery Mildew: *Sphaerotheca humuli*

Powdery mildew is the oldest of the fungal diseases affecting hops. It caused great damage in the USA when hops were grown on the east coast and was one of the problems that forced the hop industry west where powdery mildew does not occur in commercial hop yards. The disease is characterized by white fuzzy mold growing on

202

Hop aphids closeup. Photo courtesy of Larry Wright.

both sides of the leaves. If the disease proves to be persistent, it can be controlled with sulfur-based fungicides. *Important Note: If you see this disease and you live near a commercial hop growing region, please immediately notify the commercial hop organizations in your locality as it could prove disastrous to the industry.*

Hop Aphid: *Phorodon humuli*

This pest is a problem in all hop growing districts of the Northern Hemisphere except some areas in China. If uncontrolled, this insect is capable of completely destroying a crop. The soft green aphids can completely cover the underside of the leaves, sucking the life out of the plant. They can also appear later during cone formation, particularly in cooler weather, and inhabit the inner part of the cone making control next to impossible at this late phase. Black sooty mold grows on the honeydew of the aphid in hop cones and is often the reason for not picking

Aphid Sooty Mold. Photo courtesy of Dave Wills.

some vines. The aphid overwinters on various species of *Prunus* , mainly on sloe (*P. spinosa*), Damsons (*P. insititia*) and plums (*P.domestica*). The eggs are laid in the axils of the buds and hatch wingless females in the spring. They reproduce asexually, and soon produce winged females that migrate to the hop. Once on the hop the migrants produce several generations of wingless, asexual aphids that build up in large numbers throughout the summer unless controlled. The actual aphid has a very soft body and is not hard to kill, but the tall vines and abundant leaves make it difficult to effectively spray the vine and hit all the aphids. Organic insecticides such as an insecticidal soap, nicotine and diatomaceous earth work well if effectively applied. Some success can be derived via the introduction of ladybugs and lacewing predator insects as long as the predators decide to stay on the hops. The other option is to spray with a commercial insecticide such as diazinon or malathion.

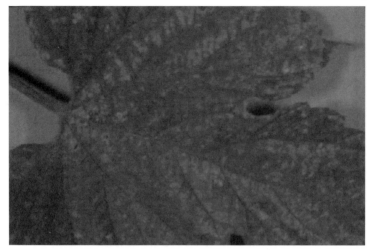

Damage to the hopleaf caused by Spider Mites.
Photo courtesy of Wyatt Cone.

Spider Mite: *Tetranychus urticae*

Spider mites are mainly a problem in hot dry climates. Females overwinter mainly in the soil or under leaves. In the spring they emerge and climb up the vines to feed on the lower sides of the leaves. Very small and just visible to the naked eye, their arrival is more evident by the existence of their fine white webs on the bottom of leaves. Mites are often not as big a problem as aphids, so control may not be necessary. Many of the same insecticides used on aphids are also effective on spider mites. The introduction of predatory mites is also proving to be a somewhat effective control measure.

Please note that most of the above pests and diseases have *humuli* in the Latin name. This means that they are specific problems on hops and do not infect or inhabit other plants. Therefore if hops do not have a history of growing

205

near your location, these problems will hopefully not exist in your area. Don't let the potential problems of growing hops stop you any more than the potential of brewing a bad batch of beer. Mainly because of the higher heat used in drying commercial hops, their full aromatic potential may be somewhat diminished. Therefore by using lower drying temperatures and hopefully organic growing conditions, homegrown hops are the best.

Which Hops Should You Grow?

If you grow bittering hops, the main problem you will have is determining the alpha acid content. You can use the information in this book as a general guide, but since your growing conditions, climate, etc. are likely to vary widely from commercial practice, so will your alpha acids. You could test brew a batch, and using the methods outlined in Chapter 8, estimate the IBUs of the beer using the taste-titration method. The problem remains however that you really need a large quantity of hops to get a really "average" alpha acid rating for the crop, and you won't have that large a quantity of hops.

So the best recommendation is to grow aroma varieties. Use them for finishing and dry hopping and not for bittering. You won't know the oil content, but if properly dried and stored, the aroma should be wonderful. And besides, you'll want to really appreciate your hop growing efforts, and that is best done with the hop character and aroma in your beer, not the simple bitterness.

Major US-Grown Varieties

Variety	Yield	Maturity	Usage	Cone Structure
Cascade	high	mid-season	aroma	elongated
Centennial	moderate	mid-season	alpha or aroma	medium, dense
Chinook	high	mid to late	alpha or aroma	long with outward bracts
Crystal	moderate	mid to late	aroma	medium, oval
Fuggle	low	early	aroma	small, light
Galena	high	mid-season	alpha	medium compact, plump
Hallertauer	low	early	aroma	loose, small, light
Liberty	moderate	mid-season	aroma	small, plump, dense
Mt. Hood	moderate	mid-season	aroma	medium, compact
N. Brewer	moderate	mid-season	alpha	medium, loose
Nugget	high	mid to late	alpha	long, tight
Perle	moderate	early	alpha/aroma	loose, medium long
Saaz	very low	early	aroma	small, light
Tettnanger	low	early	aroma	small, compact
Willamette	moderate	mid-season	aroma	medium, round, light

Bibliography

This section lists most of the reference materials used to write this book, and also contains some other pointers to interesting reading concerning hops. Since there were no "reference marks" used in the text of the book, you'll have to figure out which entry in this section relates to what part of the book, but that is usually pretty obvious. For example, if the article I've listed below concerns alpha acids or utilization, then you can assume I used it as a reference for some of the data in the chapters concerning bittering. I've also grouped them accordingly.

Most of the references listed here will, unfortunately, be hard to come by for the average brewer. This will be especially true of the various journal articles. You should check with the libraries in your local university as a best bet to finding them. If you live near a major brewery, they may allow you access to their reference library. You could also write to the publisher of the journal and ask about obtaining reprints.

With some of the references, I've included editorial comments. These are just my opinions. Lastly, I couldn't possibly have listed all the references I've read in the two years researching and writing this book, so I've just listed the more interesting ones.

General References

Hops by R.A. Neve. Published by Chapman and Hall, London, 1991. This expensive book covers a lot of ground, but is primarily a reference for the hop farmer. It has some interesting historical information, but is very short on brewing information. Most of what is presented is also presented in *Malting and Brewing Science* (same publisher). Given this book's high price, you'd be better off to invest in *Malting and Brewing Science*.

Malting and Brewing Science by Hough, Briggs, Stevens and Young. Published by Chapman and Hall, London. Second edition, 1982. This is actually a two-volume set that covers everything you ever wanted to know about brewing, usually at a very technical level. It is quite expensive, but worth it if the technical talk doesn't scare you and you really want good information. All of the hop-related topics are covered in Volume 2, so you could just get that and save some money.

The Essentials of Beer Style by Fred Eckhardt. Published by Fred Eckhardt Communications, Portland, OR, 1989. No specific hop information, but lists IBUs for a lot of commercial beers. Also has a good section on taste perception.

Zymurgy Special Issues - Hops (1990), *Classic Beer Styles* (1991) and *Gadgets* (1992). Published by the American Homebrewer's Association, Boulder CO. The *Hops* special issue is a mixed bag of good information and bad. It's worth having though as long as you can sort out what's presented. Note that I did not use any of the information directly from that issue in the preparation of this book (with the exception of the bittering formula structure), but it does contain a lot of similar information in a more abbreviated form. The *Classic Beer Styles* issue is primarily where I got the "style" guidelines for this book. Get it if you want more information on beer styles. The *Gadgets* issue has a couple of articles on how to build a hop back.

Brewing Techniques, The New Brewer and *Zymurgy* magazines have hop-related articles in them from time-to-time. *Zymurgy* leans towards the general audience and *Brewing Techniques* is more technical. *The New Brewer* is aimed at the pub and microbrewer. See ads for all of them in the back of the book.

The Classic Beer Styles Series, various authors. Published by Brewers Publications, Boulder CO. Usually these books give specific hopping recommendations for the beer style the book addresses. Two standouts are both by Terry Foster: *Pale Ale* and *Porter*.

Hop Varietal Specifications, published in various forms periodically by the hop brokers. The most useful of these is published by Hopunion USA, Inc. and is where I got a good deal of the varietal characteristics for this book. Hopunion does not sell directly to homebrewers, but some homebrew suppliers may carry their booklet. Microbrewers can request it directly.

Bittering and Utilization

An Investigation of the Relationships Between Hopping Rate, Time of Boil and Individual Alpha Acid Utilization, Irwin, Murray and Thompson. American Society of Brewing Chemists Journal, 1985, Vol. 43 No. 3.

The Fate of Humulone During Wort Boiling and Cooling, Maule. Journal of the Institute of Brewing, Vol. 72, 1966.

Practical Aspects of the Isomerization of Alpha Acids, Verzele. Proceedings of the European Brewing Convention Congress, Stockholm 1965.

Hop Substances and Yeast Behaviour, Dixon. Journal of the Institute of Brewing, Vol. 73, 1967.

Hop Isomerization, Westwood. Proceedings of the EBC Symposium on Wort Boiling and Clarification, France 1991.

Factors Affecting the Efficient Utilization of Hops, Hall. Proceedings of the EBC Congress Copenhagen 1957.

The Losses of Bitter Substances During Fermentation, Laws, McGuinness and Rennie. Journal of the Institute of Brewing, Vol. 78, 1972.

Hop Aroma and Character

Changes in Hop Oil Content and Hoppiness Potential During Hop Aging, Foster and Nickerson. ASBC Journal, 1985 Vol. 43, No. 3. Also relates to hop storage.

Chemistry of Hop Aroma in Beer, Peacock and Deinzer. ASBC Journal, 1981, Vol. 39, No. 4.

The True Value of Aroma Hops in Brewing, Kowaka, Fukuoka, Kawasaki and Asano. Proceedings of the EBC Congress, 1983.

Late-Hop Flavour, Murray, Westwood and Daoud. Proceedings of the EBC Congress, 1987.

Hop Aroma Component Profile and the Aroma Unit, Nickerson and Van Engel. ASBC Journal 1992 Vol. 50, No. 3.

A Study of the Fate of Volatile Hop Constituents in Beer, Buttery, Black, Lewis and Ling. Journal of Food Science, Volume 32, 1967.

The Microbiology of Dry Hopping, Guinard, Woodmansee, Billovits, Hanson, Gutierrez, Snider, Miranda and Lewis. Master Brewers Association of America Technical Quarterly, Vol 27, No. 3, 1990.

Hop Storage

The Effects of Storage Temperature on the Stability of the Alpha Acid Content of Baled Hops, Skinner, Hildebrand and Clarke. Journal of the Institute of Brewing, Vol. 83, 1977.

An Index of Deterioration in Hops (Humulus lupulus), Likens, Nickerson and Zimmerman. ASBC Proceedings, 1970.

Kinetics of Hop Storage, Green. Journal of the Institute of Brewing, Vol. 84, 1978.

Hop Oxidative Transforms and Control for Beer Bitterness, Rehberger and Bradee. MBAA Technical Quarterly, Vol. 12, No. 1, 1975.

Deterioration of Pelleted Hop Powders During Long-Term Storage, Wain, Baker and Laws. Journal of the Institute of Brewing, Vol. 83, 1977.

Index

A

B

Using Hops

I

N

nitrogen flushing. *See* inert gas flushing
noble hops 29, 101, 166
Northern Brewer, domestic 46. *See also* Hallertau Northern Brewer
Nugget 47

O

oast house 75
oil content rating 101, 170, 187
old hops 120
orchard ladder 201
oxidation 97
oxygen barrier. *See* barrier bags/packaging

P

pasteurization 133
pellet press 83
pellets 82, 105, 130, 141, 166, 167, 168
percent utilization. *See* utilization
Perle 30, 48
Phorodon humuli. *See* Hop Aphid
pilsner 158
Pilsner Urquell 55
pockets 77
polyethylene 107
Powdery Mildew 202
pre-isomerized pellets 84
predicting alpha acid loss 110
predicting utilization 127, 135
preservative qualities 157
Pride of Ringwood 49
Pseudoperonospora humuli. *See* Downy Mildew

Q

Questions? No answers here. See another letter

R

Rager, Jackie 134
raw hopping. *See* dry hopping

Examine the World of
Microbrewing
and
Pubbrewing

Travel the world of commercial, small-scale brewing; the realm of microbrewers and pubbrewers.

The New Brewer magazine guides you through this new industry. Its pages introduce you to marketing, finance, operations, equipment, recipes, interviews — in short, the whole landscape.

Subscribe to
The New Brewer
and become a
seasoned traveler.

No Risk Offer

Subscribe now and receive six issues. Money-back guarantee

$55 a year (U.S.)
$65 (Foreign)

Published by the Institute for Brewing Studies, PO Box 1510, Boulder, CO 80306-1510, (303) 546-6514.

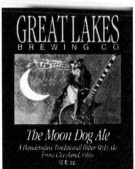

The ***New Brewer***
THE MAGAZINE FOR MICRO- AND PUB-BREWERS

HOMEBREWER?

Join the thousands of American Homebrewers Association members who read **zymurgy** — the magazine for homebrewers and beer lovers.

Every issue of **zymurgy** is full of tips, techniques, new recipes, new products, equipment and ingredient reviews, beer news, technical articles — the whole world of homebrewing. PLUS, the AHA brings members the National Homebrewers Conference, the National Homebrew Competition, the Beer Judge Certification Program, the Homebrew Club Network, periodic discounts on books from Brewers Publications and much, much more.

Photocopy and mail this coupon today to join the AHA or call now for credit card orders, (303) 546-6514.

Name _____

Address _____

City _____ State/Province _____

Zip/Postal Code _____ Country _____

Phone _____

☐ Enclosed is $29 for one full year.
   Canadian memberships are $34 US, Foreign memberships are $44 US.

☐ Please charge my credit card ☐ Visa ☐ MC

Card No. ___ — ___ — ___ Exp. Date _____

Signature _____

Make check to: American Homebrewers Association, PO Box 1510, Boulder, CO 80306 USA
Offer valid until 12/31/95.   Prices subject to change.   BP093